WAR AGAINST TERRORISM

SPECIAL FORCES IN AFGHANISTAN

2001-2003

Eric MICHELETTI

Translated from the French by Cyril Lombardini

Histoire & Collections - Paris

FIVE HUNDRED COMMANDOS TO WIN A WAR
The Coalition's Special Forces in the Afghanistan conflict

The Pentagon experts had estimated that the conflict would last all winter and would end, in the best case, by the spring of 2002. In reality, by mid-November 2001, the Taliban regime had already collapsed and its "military" units could no longer be considered as an organized force. This result had been achieved with the loss of five American lives. A magnificent victory by all accounts, a victory that was achieved by a not so subtle mix of precision ammunition, omnipotent and omnipresent air power, very well trained small groups of Special Forces soldiers and some local units trained, led and equipped by the Coalition.

In eighteen days, in the North of the country, with only four teams supported by another fifteen operators, for a grand total of no more than seventy-eight operators, the Special Forces managed to prize two thirds of the country from the Taliban's grip. That incredible result was achieved thanks to a very wide dispersion of the operators on the grounds divided into several A-Teams, each split into four detachments of three soldiers in order to cover the maximum of enemy territory. As a matter of fact, this war was won by less than five hundred Special Forces and CIA agents, who, in forty-nine days, from the moment they landed in Afghanistan to the fall of Kandahar, brought down the Taliban regime.

The "winning team": Air power and Special Forces

The combination of special operators on the ground and permanent air power above the theatre of operations made victory possible. This is a first in the history of modern warfare; if, in past conflicts, special units had managed to deal severe blows to their enemies like the *Long Range Desert Group* in Libya did against the *Afrika Korps*, the various SAS units did on different theatres of operations, the Jedburgh and others special units did in France or the Chindits against the Japanese in Burma, a classic war had never been won before by the simple action of a few hundred special forces operators.

However, this picture has to be somewhat altered; the action of this winning team would have been different without the presence on the ground of the anti-Taliban Northern Alliance in the North of the country, which had managed to survive from 1996 till 2001, not only as guerrillas, but as regular forces. In the autumn of 2001, the Alliance could field, on their two main fronts of Takhar in the northeast of the country and of the Shomali plain some forty five kilometres North of Kabul about twelve thousand fighters, some artillery pieces and some armoured vehicles (the "armoured units" were strengthened in the summer of 2001 by the delivery of dozens of T-55s and BMP-1s provided by the Russians). To those two main fronts, one must had the countless pockets of resistance in the centre of Afghanistan, which made life difficult for the Taliban and forced them to spread their forces on the ground. It is obvious that those Northern Alliance forces, difficult to esteem by Western standards, proved invaluable by their courage, their vast knowledge the country and their connections.

Resilience and experience

When the American special forces teams were infiltrated in Afghanistan in October, 2001, they had three principal types of missions to carry out: to try and set some sort of order and coordination between the various Uzbek and Tajik groups of the Northern Alliance; to try to create a Pachtoun maquis in the South; and to provide information on all the possible targets that could be subjected to American and Coalition air power. The success of these missions relied heavily on the quality of the relations between the Special Forces and the various intelligence services as well as on the confidence they would manage to win from their Afghan contacts on the ground.

As we have already seen, those missions were all a success. This was due to the now vast experience of the American Special Forces in the field of unconventional warfare, specifically in the training of indige-

Fire and Movement exercise for USAF Combat Control Team operators. The CCTs have played an instrumental role in the campaign.
(USAF Picture)

nous forces, to the courage of the Northern Alliance fighters and to the complete air supremacy of the USA that was never once challenged during the conflict. As a matter of fact, this war could almost be called "special force centric" as during the first five months the majority of the military operations had been undertaken by special units. The middle of December 2001 and the failure of the operations around Tora Bora to reach their advertised aim saw the conduct of the war being taken over by CENTCOM; this was followed by the arrival of conventional units on the ground in Afghanistan about a month later.

In March 2002, *Operation Anaconda* marked the end of the "SF only" part of the war. The "Green Army" (conventional forces) was now back in the driving seat. However, the special units were still on the ground and very active as was seen during *Anaconda* when no less than seventy-two Special Forces teams were sent ahead of the regular units to man a string of observation posts and to patrol the area of operations.

These operations once more demonstrated the value of real time information that mostly transited through US Navy P-3C Orion and UAVs

of all descriptions. With the assistance of those manned and unmanned aircrafts that were permanently circling over their heads, the commandos on the ground could unleash tactical air power at will on any enemy and thus helped securing victory in a geographical area where difficult communications has been a key factor for all warriors for centuries.

During those operations, the SF troopers realized that their enemies tended to be well trained and to fight until they were killed or severely wounded. The Americans also discovered that the Taliban relied heavily on cellular telephones as tactical radios, the main commanders even being provided with state-of-the-art satellite telephone suitcases-cum computers; to make matters worse, the American also found out that the Taliban even used the very same radio sets they used, the last generation PRC-117!

Alongside the Americans, other Coalition Special Forces played an important role in the final operations, in particular the British SAS and SBS, the Australian SAS and the Norwegian, Danish and German commandos.

The war turns conventional.

At the beginning of September, 2002, the staff officers of the *Joint Special Operations Command* (JSOC) openly stated that, as far as special operations units were concerned, the campaign against Ben Laden was over. For them, Ussama Ben Laden had been killed during the Tora Bora bombardments in December 2001. This theory was confirmed, according to some, by the absence of radio intercepts or of any other sign for that matter proving his existence in the Afghan mountains of the South of the country (which had already been finely combed by the military) or in Pakistan. For JSOC, the presence of special forces in Afghanistan could not be justified any more, and conventional units were considered as amply sufficient to hunt down the last Taliban and terrorists and to search the different regions of the country that were still thought to pose some form of threat.

Eric Micheletti

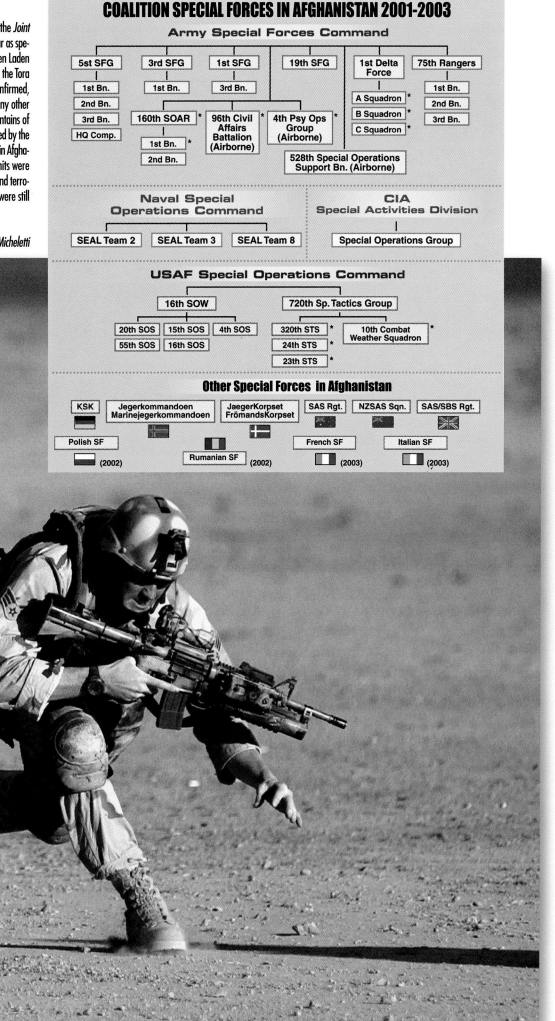

COALITION SPECIAL FORCES IN AFGHANISTAN 2001-2003

Army Special Forces Command

5st SFG	3rd SFG	1st SFG	19th SFG	1st Delta Force	75th Rangers
1st Bn.	1st Bn.	3rd Bn.			1st Bn.
2nd Bn.				A Squadron *	2nd Bn.
3rd Bn.	160th SOAR *	96th Civil Affairs Battalion (Airborne) *	4th Psy Ops Group (Airborne) *	B Squadron *	3rd Bn.
HQ Comp.	1st Bn. *			C Squadron *	
	2nd Bn.		528th Special Operations Support Bn. (Airborne)		

Naval Special Operations Command

SEAL Team 2	SEAL Team 3	SEAL Team 8

CIA Special Activities Division

Special Operations Group

USAF Special Operations Command

16th SOW			720th Sp. Tactics Group	
20th SOS	15th SOS	4th SOS	320th STS *	10th Combat Weather Squadron *
55th SOS	16th SOS		24th STS *	
			23th STS *	

Other Special Forces in Afghanistan

KSK	Jegerkommandoen Marinejegerkommandoen	JaegerKorpset FrömandsKorpset	SAS Rgt.	NZSAS Sqn.	SAS/SBS Rgt.

Polish SF	Rumanian SF	French SF	Italian SF
(2002)	(2002)	(2003)	(2003)

Year 2001

October the 7th and 8th,2001. Military operations by American and British armed forces in Afghanistan begin against Taliban and "Al-Qaida" targets. USAF, USN and USMC aircrafts, as well as Americans and British Tomahawk missiles hit thirty objectives. American and British Special Forces are flown to different locations around Afghanistan, Pakistan, Uzbekistan, Turkmenistan, Tajikistan, as well as on to the USS Kitty Hawk.

October 9.USAF,USN and USMC aircrafts, as well as Tomahawk missiles are used to attack thirteen targets in Afghanistan, including a surface-to-air (SAM) site near Kandahar and a headquarters near Mazar-e-Sharif. At the same time, USAF C-17s air-drop food supplies on population concentrations in the South of Afghanistan.

October 10. Air operations go on all night. The USAF strikes six targets during daylight hours, whereas British tactical air reconnaissance aircraft undertake several missions over Afghanistan. This is only a beginning for the British as RAF tankers will participate in air operations over Afghanistan until the summer of 2002

October 11. American aircraft and USN Tomahawk missiles strike seven targets.

October 12. American aircrafts attack seventeen targets and Tomahawk missiles are launched by a Royal Navy submarine.

October 14. Seven targets are hit, while propaganda leaflets begin to be released over Afghanistan by USSOCOM aircrafts.

October 15. Twelve targets are hit and food rations are air-dropped by C-17s flying in from Germany.

October 16. USAF, USN and USMC aircraft bombard twelve different targets. The air drop of food rations continues.USS Kitty Hawk, with Special Forces and helicopters onboard, approaches the Pakistani coast.

October 17. USAF, USN and USMC aircraft bombard about twenty different targets. Six cruise missiles strike Kabul. For the first time, an AC-130 "Gunship" based in Uzbekistan provides fire support to anti-Taliban forces in the North of the country. Propaganda leaflets are still dropped by the thousands and a Commando Solo C130 begins to emit broadcasts that are favourable to the coalition. The Talibans try to loosen the Northern Alliance grip on the Mazar-e-Sharif area. American special operation units, mainly Rangers and Delta Force, land on the Pakistani airports of Dalbandin and Samungli.

October 18. Eighteen targets are hit, while the air drop of food rations continues. A Special Forces helicopter crashes in Pakistan, wounding two.

October 19. American Special Forces undertake two heliborne operations in the South of Afghanistan to try and cut the road connecting the cities of Kandahar to Herat. In the meantime, American aircrafts strike fifteen different targets. Special Forces lose two helicopters. AFSOC undertakes a massive leaflet dropping operation on several Afghan cities and urbanized areas. In the same night, MC-130Hs, having taken off from Oman, parachute hundred of Rangers in the southwest of Kandahar, under the protection of AC-130s. At the same time, Delta Force troopers helicoptered from Pakistan launch an operation to try to capture either mullah Omar or Ben Laden. In both cases, operations are compromised by watchful Taliban and the American commandos choose to abort the operations. All those units are then extracted by MH-53J Pave Low helicopters.

October 20. Six different targets are attacked. The leaflet dropping missions and the broadcasting of coalition propaganda continues. An MH-53J crashes North of Kandahar. For the first time, at least officially, a Predator UAV fires a series of missiles against strategic targets.

October 21. Eight targets are attacked, C-17s keep on with the parachuting of food rations and the AFSOC leaflet-dropping

missions and broadcasting of coalition propaganda continue. Two AC-130 strafe targets around Kabul. Special Forces teams are infiltrated into the southwest of Kandahar, one of their helicopters crashes.

October 22. Eleven targets are hit by American aircrafts. The RAF continues its reconnaissance and refuelling operations. Advised by Green Berets teams and Air Force commandos,the Northern Alliance troops start their offensive in the Darae Souf valley, as well as in the Balkh and Samangan provinces.

October 23. USAF, USN and USMC aircraft bombard five targets. All night bombardments are carried out on targets in the Kabul region, west of Herat and around Mazar-e-Sharif. Reinforcements for the Talibans stream in from Pakistan's tribal zones.

October 24. Nine targets are hit, and the dropping of leaflets and food rations goes on in numerous regions. Helicopters of the 16th Special Operations Wing provide the various Tajik guerrilla movements stemming from the Bamian and Ghowr provinces with weapons, ammunition and soldiers.

October 25. USAF, USN and USMC aircrafts bombard ten targets. The dropping of leaflets and food rations continues. South of Kabul, an anti-Taliban group inserted by American helicopters and led by the Pachtoun leader Abdul Haq is surrounded by Taliban. The leader is arrested and executed. This operation is considered as a failure for the United States in their dealings with the anti-Taliban groups.

October 26. The air interdiction of Taliban targets goes on, involving the strike of an undisclosed number of objectives. There are now several hundred American and British Special Forces troops in Afghanistan.

October 27. USAF, USN and USMC aircraft bombard about twenty targets.

October 28. Numerous air operations in the North of the country. An American heliborne operation with the aim of dropping partisans of the king and tasked with the negotiating of a possible reu-

AFGHANISTAN

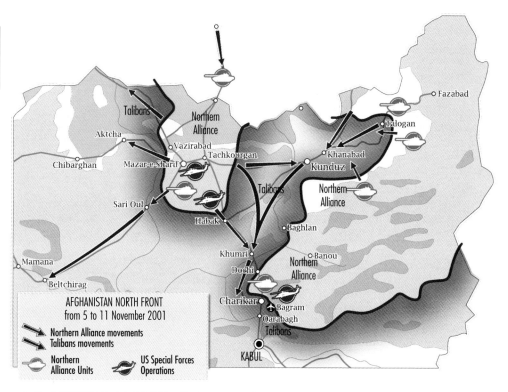

nification of Pachtounes tribes fails because they are quickly surrounded and taken prisoner.

October 29. Six targets are attacked by American aircraft and the dropping of leaflets goes on. The Commando Solo C130 maintains its AM and SW broadcasting operations.

October 30. Thirteen targets are bombarded; the dropping of leaflets by AFSOC aircraft and food rations by C17 goes on. South of Kandahar, in Babi Sahib, an airborne and heliborne operation is conducted by about one hundred Rangers whose mission is to form a safety perimeter while a Delta Forces group "takes down" several buildings supposed to shelter Oussama Ben Laden and his staff. More than a dozen helicopters from the 160th Special Operations Aviation Regiment, as well as four AC-130s, are used for this operation. It is a failure: the buildings are empty, the American Special Forces lose three KIA, nine others are wounded, and a CH-53 helicopter crashes.

October 31. Bombardments intensify, the American commanders having decided to break the Taliban lines of defence in the Mazar-e-Sharif region as well as in the Bagram region near Kabul. USAF, USN and USMC aircraft bombard twenty different targets and the leaflet dropping operation goes on.

November 1st. Bombardment of eight targets with RAF tactical air reconnaissance and refuelling support. In almost a month of bombardment, the Talibans have lost most of their military infrastructure and most of their heavy equipment. Of the hundred and fifty tanks which they were supposed to operate, more than a hundred have been destroyed, the rest are deployed in fixed, hull down positions. By that time, most of the artillery pieces still in position have also been destroyed.

November 2. Nine targets are attacked. Due to severe weather conditions, a Special Forces helicopter crashes in Afghanistan without loss, and a CIA Predator UAV is reported as missing during a mission.

November 3. The bombardments continue but the number of sorties is not made public. The Americans decide to commit more of their air power to the support of general Dostom's Uzbek forces. USAF B-52s, B-1Bs and F-15s and USN and USMC F-18s do round-the-clock bombardment of the Taliban positions controlling the access to Mazar-e-Sahrif in the northwest of the country.

November 4. Bombardments on the "northern front" continue, the exact number of targets hit is kept secret; at the same time, the air dropping of food rations goes on in several areas. An American CH-53 helicopter is hit by Taliban ground fire and crashes in the Chaghi district in Baluchistan, causing the death of four Special Forces operators.

November 5. Five targets are attacked. Radio broadcasts are resumed.

November 6. USAF, USN and USMC aircraft bombard a certain number of objectives. The air dropping of leaflets and the radio broadcasts are maintained.

November 7. American aircraft maintain an unrelenting pres-

sure on Taliban in the Mazar-e-Sharif zone. Besides B-52s, C-130s drop 7 tons BLU-82B bombs. Vehicle columns loaded with Talibans, Pakistani volunteers and numerous volunteers of Arabic origin are systematically attacked and destroyed. US Special Forces helicoptered in advance along the Taliban's infiltration routes achieve brilliant results in their FAC (Forward Air Control) missions, "painting" dozens of targets with their Tactical Laser Designators.

November 8. Fourteen targets are bombarded. Leaflets are released over Afghanistan's main cities. The Sholgera district, less than seventy kilometres from Mazar-e-Sharif, falls without a fight.

November 9. American commanders accentuate the bombardment missions in the North of the country in support of the anti-Taliban coalition.

November 10. More than one hundred targets in the North of the country are bombarded. Leaflets are still dropped in many areas and radio broadcasts are maintained.

November 11. Fall of Mazar-e-Sharif, often considered as the strategic city of the North.

USAF, USN and USMC aircraft bombard a great number of targets, including several fleeing Talibans convoys. However, a certain number of the Taliban fighters along with some of their allies manage to retreat on to Kunduz, more to the East. The Mazar-e-Sharif airport is taken. A few hours later, the first AFSOC C-130s and helicopters, arriving from Uzbekistan, land on the runway. Discreetly, the first Special Forces light vehicles cross into Afghanistan at Termez in the middle of the tanks and APCs of Dostom's mechanized "brigade" which was, supposedly, made up of volunteer soldiers from the regular Uzbek Army.

All the while, all the Taliban fighters who surrender are systematically executed by general Dostom's Uzbek soldiers.

During the Spring of 2002, on the Kandahar air base, 45 Commando Royal Marines belonging to *Task Force Jacana* return from a search operation.
(MOD Picture)

The road towards Kabul is now free for the forces of Dostom the American air power having annihilated the Talibans column on the run.

However, after intense discussions between various members o the American government and the US general staff, it is decide that Dostom's army will not penetrate into the Afghan capital because a blood bath would have almost certainly followed.

Washington then resolves itself to choosing the Tajik's Norther Alliance which used to be under the undisputed leadership of th recently assassinated "major" Massoud. In a few hours, fror 0900(local time) to 1400 hours precisely, the USAF the bomber literally crush the Talibans positions as well as those of their allie At the same time, Tadjik forces reach an agreement with the loc. Taliban leaders to let them have the unimpaired use of the Kabu road.

November 12. During the night, the Taliban leaves Kabul an loses control of Herat, in the West of the country. American air powe continues the bombardments of the last Taliban positions and "A Qaida's " camps. A pair of Russian built helicopters belonging t the CIA covertly inserts several teams of operators in the suburb of Kabul in order to retrieve as many embarrassing documents a possible pertaining to former links between US politicians and th Taliban.

November 13. USAF, USN and USMC aircraft bombard variou objectives, whereas the AFSOC releases pamphlets on cities that ar still in the hands of the Taliban. The Northern Alliance forces ente Kabul under the protection of two Russian MI-24 helicopters repain ted in Afghan colours. The provinces of Balkh, Fariab, Jauzhan Samangan and Sar-e-Pol fall into the hands of Dostom's troops. A the same time, in the South of the country, a certain number o

in the South of Ghazni. The pace of air operations remains relentless. Ghazni's airport is used to its full capacity and it rapidly becomes a forward operating base for American Special Forces. In the Northeast, around the city of Kunduz, several thousands Taliban, Pakistani volunteers and Arabic fighters are surrounded by the forces of the Northern Alliance as well as by General Dostom's units. None of those two forces are spoiling for a fight and they are both happy to wait for American air power to soften up their opponent's positions. This situation remains unchanged until November 24.

November 18. USAF, USN and USMC aircraft bombard various objectives in the South of the country. Targets are now becoming scarce since the Taliban have, by now, abandoned all their heavy equipment and are hiding in the mountains.

November 19. Approximately twenty targets are designated to American aircrafts by ground forces. Several airdrops of leaflets are undertaken in the Northeast and the Southeast of the country.

November 20. USAF, USN and USMC aircraft bombard various objectives in the South and the northeast of the country.

November 21. Bombardments continue while rations and leaflets are dropped in the centre of the country.

November 22. Bombardments continue while rations and leaflets are dropped in the centre of the country.

November 24. The air operations and bombardments continue in support of US Special Forces in pursuit of the Taliban. At the same time, around the Taliban resistance pocket of Kunduz, and after lengthy negotiations, the Northern Alliance forces finally decide to attack — while Dostom forces' merely watch the more than three thousand defenders of the pocket which will finally fall the next day.

Left. In March 2002, on the road to Gardez, a US Special Forces Group Humvee patrol opens the way for other Army units.
(Paula Bronstein/Getty/SIPA-Press Picture)

Below.
December 2002, in the Landa Khel village. Staff Sergeant Robert Brooks and another member of the 82nd Airborne Division erect the antenna of a satellite communication system.
(DOD Picture)

the 15th MEU (Marine Expeditionary Unit SOC) (Special Operations Capable) from their bases in Pakistan to camp Rhino.

November 27. USAF, USN and USMC aircraft bombard various objectives in the South, and especially the mountains of Meelawa, South of Jalalabad, where the soon-to-be-famous Tora Bora sector is located. Indeed, according to the Pakistani intelligence services, hundreds of Taliban fighters and "Al-Qaida" members including their leader, have taken refuge in this region.

November 28. The air operations and bombardments continue in support of US Special Forces in pursuit of the Taliban; leaflets are still released on a large scale.

November 29. The same types of air operations are undertaken in support of US special units.

November 30. USAF, USN and USMC aircraft bombard various objectives.

December 1st. The same types of air operations are undertaken in support of US special units. American, British, Australian and New Zealand Special Forces are regrouped on Jalalabad's airport. They start preparing for a possible operation in the Tora Bora area.

December 2. USAF, USN and USMC aircraft bombard various objectives and AFSOC planes release leaflets and broadcast propaganda radio programs.

December 3. The same types of air missions are undertaken.

December 4. USAF, USN and USMC aircraft bombard various objectives a soldier of the Army Special Forces is killed by a B-52 bombardment in the North of Kandahar. Four British SBS/SAS are wounded in a collision in front of Tora Bora.

December 5. The same types of air missions are undertaken mostly support to American units and to drop leaflets.

December 6. USAF, USN and USMC aircraft bombard various objectives and kill by mistake three members of the US special forces, Staff Sergeant Brian Cody Prosser (aged 28), Master Sergeant Jefferson Donald Davis (aged 39), and Sergeant First Class Daniel Henry Petithory (aged 32).

December 7. USAF, USN and USMC aircraft bombard various objectives. After two days of negotiations, the Taliban of the provinces of Helmand, Kandahar and Kaboul agree to surrender.

From December the 8th until January the 1st, 2002. Continuation of air operations led by various USAF, USN and USMC aircraft, in particular in theTora Bora region, where about 2 000 tons of bombs, including several BLU-82, are released. Leaflet dropping stops, but radio broadcasts from the air continue. About two hundred Marines from the 58th Operational Group, along with Australian SAS, take control of the airport of Kandahar.

December 11. A USAF B-1B bomber crashes to the sea, about fifty kilometres from its Diego Garcia base. The crew is rescued.

December 15. The last fighting is reported in the Tora Bora region, in the east of Afghanistan. In fact, the Afghan troops engaged for the occasion allowed their opponents to pass through their lines after negotiations, something that rendered the Coalition's Special Forces furious. Only two hundred corpses, mostly victims of bombardments, were found and about sixty people were arrested. Later, it was realized that these prisoners were in fact only recently arrived Pakistani volunteers, without any real links with " Al-Qaida".

December 17. Two C-130 Hercules approaching the Kandahar airport are hit by SA-7 missiles.

December 21. The temporary Afghan government takes office in Kabul. Royal Marines of 40 Commando RM land in Bagram and begin to patrol the area.

December 25. The US Air Force attacks a group of buildings held by the Taliban, in Tori Khel.

Pachtounes tribes and Taliban groups are "turned" with the help of dollars generously distributed by the local CIA agents and they rebel around Kandahar, the city of mullah Omar. The order is given to Taliban units scattered around the country to concentrate around the northeast, near Kunduz, and in the south, near Kandahar.

A rescue operation is launched by Delta Force to save eight western aid workers of an NGO held hostage.

November 14. The ground attacks of USAF, USN and USMC aircraft are now mostly directed against targets in the South of Afghanistan. The city of Jalalabad, controlling the main road towards Pakistan, falls into the hands of anti-Taliban Pachtoun groups. A team of British SBS is inserted by helicopters on to Bagram's airport, in order to seize the installations "right under the afghan troops' noses".

November 15. The ground attacks of USAF, USN and USMC aircrafts continue in the North and the southeast of Afghanistan around Gardez. "Psychological" air operations take place around Kabul and in the southeast of the country. Talibans abandon the city of Ghazni, for fear of being surrounded by the Northern Alliance which is coming from Kabul and the American Special Forces which were helicoptered on the outskirts of the town, towards Kandahar.

November 16. USAF, USN and USMC aircraft bombard various objectives.

November 17. Targets are no longer fixed by briefings and opportunity bombing starts on different targets like Taliban convoys

November 25. While air actions continue, the Northern Alliance delegation flies from Bagram bound for Berlin. CH-53 helicopters from the Marine Corps insert an important group of Marine Recon on Bolangi's airstrip, about fifty kilometres southwest of Kandahar, in order to recce the site which will serve as a Forward Operation Base for the Marines. This base will soon be known by the name of camp Rhino.

November 26. USAF, USN and USMC aircraft bombard various objectives in the South, including the city of Kandahar. Throughout the day, helicopters from LHA-5 *USS Peleliu* insert Marines from

Year 2002

January 2. American air power concentrates on several terrorist camps, in the southeast of Afghanistan, near Khost.

January 3. American aircraft attack a group located near the Zhawar Kili caves. American Special Forces Sergeant Nathan Ross (aged 31) is killed in a firefight. He is the first American soldier killed in combat in Afghanistan.

January 5. USAF, USN and USMC aircraft bombard antiaircraft positions near Khost.

January 7. USAF, USN and USMC aircraft bombard different sites near Zhawar Kili, whereas AC-130s provides air support to the operations in the mountains around Khost.

January 8. Air operations continue around Zhawar Kili. Taking off from Jacobabad's base, a USMC KC-130 crashes in Pakistan: the seven crew members are killed.

From the 9th until the 13th of January. Series of air operations in Zhawar Kili's zone, with bombardments and close air support for troops in contact.

January 11. Marines of the 15th MEU are replaced in Rhino camp by the soldiers of the 101st air Assault Division.

January 17. For lack of targets, the rhythm of air operations is greatly reduced.

January 20. A USMC CH-53E crashes sixty kilometres from Bagram: two crew members are killed.

January 23. American ground units attack two areas, North of Kandahar, where " Al-Qaida " members, have been located. AC-130s of the AFSOC destroy an ammunition dump.

January 24. Special Forces supported by AC-130s launch an airmobile operation against a camp supposedly occupied by "Al-Qaida's " members, two hundred kilometres North of Kandahar. About ten opponents are killed and twenty seven are arrested. A Special Forces operator is wounded.

January 27. US Special forces and Delta Force operators assault the Kandahar hospital in order to neutralize "Al-Qaida " fighters who had refused to surrender.

January 28. A CH-47 Chinook helicopter crashes while undertaking a tactical mission near Khost. Fourteen crewmembers and passengers are wounded.

January 30. Fighting erupts between various pro governmental militia.

February 3. The first elements of the 3rd Battalion, Princess Patricia's Canadian Light Infantry arrive in Kandahar. Canadian *Operation Apollo* begins.

February 4. Officially, American Special Forces leave Afghanistan, the political situation having been judged by Washington as quiet enough.

February 7. Having surrounded and searched the Zhawar Kili's zone, American units continue ground operations.

February 16. A light vehicle belonging to the Australian SAS explodes on a land mine in the southeast of the country, causing the death of an SAS sergeant.

February 21. An MH-47 Chinook of the 160th "Night stalkers" SOAR with eight Army Special Forces operators and two Air Force Pararescuemen onboard crashes in the Philippines.

March 1st. Beginning of *operation Anaconda* in the southern region against "Al-Qaida" elements. The following units take part in this major operation: the 101st air Assault Division, the 10th Mountain Division, the 13th and 26th MEU, some Canadian units, more than five hundred Afghan fighters paid and equipped by the Americans and trained by the Coalition's Special Forces. The USAF commits ten B-52 and B-1B bombers and the US Navy deploys F / A-18 Hornet from the aircraft carrier USS John C. Stennis. For the first time, French Mirage 2000 Ds and Super-Etendards participate in the air operations. An American Special Forces operator is killed.

March 3. American air power including AC-130 provides tactical air support to ground troops. Intense fighting erupt around the caves of the Shah-e-Kot mountains valley at altitudes ranging from 2,500 meters to 3,600 meters. These engagements are very vio-

Above, left. Task Force Devil in action during Operation Mangoose that was carried out in January 2003 in the Adi Ghar mountains. (DOD Picture)

Above right. Remaining faithful to their "dune buggy" vehicles the US Navy SEALs deployed some of those troubled vehicle to the desert-like parts of Afghanistan. That deploymen was not a resounding success and the Japanese SUV and Humvees remained the favourite mode of transportation (US Navy Picture

lent and the Coalition troops encounter severe difficulties making progress. During operations around Gardez, a CH-47 inserting a group of American soldiers is shot down by ground fire.

March 4. In two days of severe combat operations, seven American Special Forces operators are killed: Technical Sergeant John A. Chapman (aged 36), Senior Airman Jason D. Cunningham aged 26 years), Navy SEAL Neil C. Robert (aged 32), and four green berets, PFC Matthew A. Commons (aged 21), Sergeant Bradley S . Crose (aged 27), Sergeant Philip J. Svitak (aged 31), an Marc A. Anderson (aged 30); around thirty people are wounded in action and fifty Afghan government soldiers are also killed.

March 5. Operations concentrate around the Shakit-Kot zone Reinforcements from the101st supported by Army AH64 Apache attack helicopters and Marine Corps Sea Cobras are sent in to support those operations.

March 9. Poor weather slows down *operation Anaconda*. A armoured column with nine hundred fighters of the Northern Alliance, which now forms the government armed forces, reaches the Gardez area to support Coalition forces.

March 10. The American command in Afghanistan announces the end of combat operations in the Shakit-Kot zone and declares that air bombardments will continue.

March 17. End of *operation Anaconda*. Great Britain announces that Royal Marine from 45 Commando group will participate in operations against the Talibans and " Al-Qaida" resistance pockets.

March 20. US Special Forces launch a night attack on Khost airport.

March 23. The advanced elements of 45 Commando Group lands in Bagram.

March 27. Intensification of air and ground patrols around Khost where" Al-Qaida " and Taliban elements could have been able to regroup.

March 28. In Kandahar Navy SEAL Chief Hospital Corpsman Matthew J. Middle (aged 35) is killed during an exercise which he was commanding.

March 29. Since the beginning of *operation Enduring Freedom,* the air forces of the Coalition have made 36 564 sorties and released 21 737 munitions of all kinds. Royal Marines of 45 Commando RM officially begin their search operations of different cave networks.

April 1st. The first combat echelon of 45 Commando RM arrives in Afghanistan.

April 10. The last elements of 45 Commando RM land in Bagram.

April 14. Beginning of *operation Ptarmigan* with units of 45 Commando group.

April 15. Near Kandahar, a US National Guard F-16 bombards a group of Canadian soldiers belonging to the 3rd Battalion of the Princess Patricia's Light Infantry by mistake: four Canadian infantrymen are killed.

April 17. End of *operation Ptarmigan* which is concluded with no British losses.

April 30. Beginning of *operation Snipe* led by units from 45 Commando RM. Their mission is to search a wide mountainous zone.

May 8. The British commando group discovers and destroys a series of "Al-Qaida" arms caches. *Operation Snipe* continues.

May 12. End of *operation Snipe.*

May 16. Beginning of *operation Condor* in which American units including Green Berets of the 5th SFG participate, alongside British SAS and SBS, Australian SAS and Afghan troops of the temporary government. Australian SAS engage and kill several Tali-

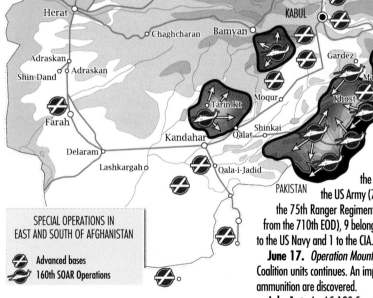

SPECIAL OPERATIONS IN
EAST AND SOUTH OF AFGHANISTAN

Advanced bases
160th SOAR Operations

ban fighters.

May 19. US Special Force Sergeant Gene Arden Vance (aged 38), is killed in action during *operation Condor.*

May 21. End of *operation Condor.*

May 22. Fire fight between Royal Marines and supposed "Al-Qaida" members.

May 23. Combined operation between Royal Marine and 5th SFG operators against buildings sheltering "Al-Qaida's " elements.

May 28. Beginning of *operation Buzzard* in the Khost region involving Royal Marine and Army Special Forces units.

June 4. *Operation Buzzard* continues.

June 12. An AFSOC MC-130 crashes at night near Gardez. Three crew members are killed in the accident, Technical Sergeant Sean M. Corlew (aged 37), Staff Sergeant Anissa A. Shero (aged 31) belonging to the Air Force, as well as Army Sergeant First Class

Peter P. Tycz (aged 32). Another seven servicemen are wounded.

June 16. To this day, 30 American soldiers have been killed in Afghanistan (14 in action), as well as 4 Canadians (friendly fire) and 1 Australian. Among the American losses, 16 belonged to the US Army (7 Special Forces operators, 5 from the 75th Ranger Regiment, 1 from the 160th SOAR (A), 3 from the 710th EOD), 9 belonged to the USMC, 2 to the USAF, 2 to the US Navy and 1 to the CIA.

June 17. *Operation Mountain Lion* involving American and Coalition units continues. An important number of weapons and ammunition are discovered.

July 1st. An AC-130 Spectre of the 16th Special Operations Wing opens fire on the village of Kakrakai, killing 58 civilians and wounding another120.

July 6. The Afghan vice-president and the Minister of civil engineerings Maji Abdul Qadir and their two bodyguards are murdered.

July 9. End of *Operation Buzzard* for the British contingent. 45 Commando RM, 59 Independent Commando Squadron Royal Engineers, a detachment of the Commando Logistic Regiment,105 mm Light guns of 7 Battery Royal Artillery and helicopters of 27 Squadron were involved in that operation.

July 10. Units of the 82nd Airborne replace those of the 101st air Assault that have by then been in Afghanistan for four straight months.

July 20. Several thousand British soldiers return to the United

Kingdom, leaving only a few staff members and some logistics teams.

July 26. Several elements of Task Force 11 operating in the Pakistani tribal zones are killed during several fire fights in this region. This TF is made up of American Special Forces and Pakistani agents which main mission is to undertake reconnaissance missions from Pakistan.

July 31. The Afghan president, Ahmid Karzaï is nearly killed in a car bomb attack.

August 11. Rangers, green berets and elements of the 82nd airborne division belonging to Task Force Panther undertake a search operation in the Paktia province.

August 16. The American command launches *operation Mountain Sweep,* following *operation Mountain Lion;* more than 2 000 soldiers forming Combined Joint Task Force 180 are deployed in the South of Khost and Gardez.

September 1st. After more than a week of *operation Mountain Sweep,* the first phases turn out to be disappointing in spite of the massive commitment of the soldiers on the ground and of an important air support. In Paktia, another operation, *Champion Strike,* continues involving several hundreds 82nd Airborne paratroopers and Rangers of the 75th Rangers regiment. At that time, some 8 000 American soldiers are operating in Afghanistan, and another thousand are operating in Pakistan along the border between the two countries.

September 5. A terrorist attack in Kabul kills 29, and another one, in Kandahar, is directed against president Karzaï's car. During the exchange of fire, the Delta Force protection detail of the Afghan president kills two Afghan bodyguards who were also in charge of protecting Karzaï.

September 18. During *Operation Mountain Sweep,* Green Berets and Rangers capture seven suspected Taliban northwest of Khost. On the whole, the results of this operation, when compared with the level of forces deployed, are disappointing.

September 20. An American advanced post near Lwara, is surrounded and attacked with rockets. Bagram based troops and Marine Corps F/A-18A/D and USN F/A-18 Hornets air support are finally necessary to relieve this forward position.

October 2. Governmental forces sweep the forces of a dissident commander from the northeast of Gardez.

October 11. To help the Kabul government, the 3rd Battalion of the 505th Parachute Infantry Regiment is deployed in the Khost area to disarm the troops of warlord Pasha Khan. Initially in favour of the American, he had by then turned into an open opponent of the new government.

October 13. Three American advanced posts north of Khost, in Lewara (180 km southwest of Kabul), and near Gardez, are simultaneously attacked by rocket and light weapon. An 160th SOAR Chinook is also damaged.

October 27. An already very tense situation between general Dostom's soldiers and those of general Atta degenerates into fights in the region of Shulgara.

November 4. Coalition forces report taking fire in Khost, Orgun and Shkin.

November 7. Rangers' positions in the east of the country are attacked with light weapon. An A-10 Warthog and Apache helicopters provide the light infantrymen with close air support, firing 30 mm cannon rounds and rockets.

November 14. Harassment operations against American positions in Lwara and Gardez. The intervention of Bagram based aircrafts and of *USS Belleau Wood* AV-8B Harriers relieves the pressure on the American positions.

2003 events

On January 27 and 28 near Spin Boldak, in the South of Afghanistan near the Pakistani border, a series of gun fights

opposes American forces, among which units of the 82nd Airborne, and governmental troops to an important group of Afghans Taliban. The US command considers that it is the most important operation since *Anaconda* in March, 2002 in the Paktia province and it brings in heavy air support in the form of B-1B, AC-130, and F-16 (among which some belonging to the Royal Norwegian Air Force). About twenty gunmen belonging to Gulbuddin Hekmaktyar's fundamentalist movement Hezb e-Islami, are killed in the mountains of Adir Ghar.

February 19. *Operation Viper* begins in the valley of Bagharn. This valley is situated in a mountainous zone of the Hemand province in the northwest of the Kandahar air base. The purpose of this operation is to search the various villages and, if possible, to find weapons and signs of Taliban and "Al Qaida" presence. Several units of the 82nd Airborne Division are involved in this operation among which the 2nd Battalion of the 504th Parachutes Infantry Regiment (2 / 504th PIR which operated alongside Civilians Affairs units.

March 5. The miniature "Matilda" robot of company C of the 27th battalion of Fort Bragg capable of operating in underground passages is put in service in tunnels around Bagram in order to locate traps, mines and explosives.

March 20. Beginning of *Operation Valiant Strike* in the mountains of Sami Ghar, about 130 kilometres east of Kandahar. The American deploy several units comprising special forces, CCTs, the 504th Parachutes Infantry Regiment of the 82nd Airborne Division, and several Rumanian units, numbering almost 600 soldiers in total. This operation was launched on the evidence of information gathered during the interrogation of Khalid Shaikh Mohammed, one of Ben Laden's lieutenants arrested on March 1st in Pakistan. Nine Afghans suspected of being in connection with Taliban are detained as a direct result of this operation and numerous small calibre ammunitions, mortar shell and rockets are discovered.

On March 25, the 504th PIR launches *operation Deser*

Above, left. January 2003; during *Operation Mangoose*, a team belonging to A Company 504th Parachute Infantry Regiment (PIR) undertaking the reconnaissance of a cave system that had been identified as a potential Taliban weapons dump. *(DOD Picture)*

Above right. A 711th Special Operations Squadron MC-130E Combat Talon loadmaster checks on the approach of an HH-60G Pace Hawk helicopter during a mid-air refuelling over Afghanistan. *(USJFCOM Picture)*

Lion in the mountains of Kohe Safi near Bagram air base. Acting on specific information, this zone, which had been searched only a few weeks before soon reveals two arms caches holding a certain number of ammunitions including mortar shell and107 mm rockets, even though the hiding site was only located five kilometres away from the base. Everything is immediately destroyed in situ by mine clearance experts.

March 30. Two Special Forces are killed and another wounded during a patrol in the province of Helmand, near Geresk. Their all terrain vehicle is ambushed by four gunmen who immediately flee the area on a motorcycle. This incident arose two days after a Red Cross hydraulic engineer was shot dead near Kandahar. At the same time, a force consisting of several hundred governmental soldiers with their US Special Forces advisors operates in the Uruzgan province in search of a Taliban column.

April 18. During *Operation Carpathian Mountains*, near Qalat in the Kabul province, Rumanian soldiers of the 812th infantry regiment locate a very important weapons cache in two different caves. A few days before, in the Faryab province in northwest of the country, governmental forces had discovered eighteen weapons caches for a total amounting to more than 200 tons of military hardware.

April 24. A CH-47 Chinook helicopter which was participating in *Operation Vigilant Guardian*, under the command of Combined Task Force 82, has to make an emergency landing near Spin Boldak. The crew removes all the sensitive equipment and blows the helicopter up.

Between March 23 and April 25, the US Army kills ten and wound seven gunmen.

April 27. Two American soldiers are killed in the Shkin region, southeast of Kabul, in a gun fight against about twenty gunmen who then flee towards neighbouring Pakistan. Three of the aggressors are killed.

An AFSOC Parajumper deployed in Afghanistan. For more details about these units, see the chapter about the AFSOC starting on page 84.

On September 22, 2001, with utmost discretion, several green berets of the 5th Special Force Group landed on the tarmac of the Khanabad base, not far from the city of Karchi in Uzbekistan, less than a hundred and eighty kilometres of the Afghani border. Some of them knew this place well because they had already come here in 1999 to train and some even spoke Uzbek and Tajik.

Ten days later, a strong Special Forces detachment, which included elements of the headquarters and headquarters company as well as various battalions of the 5th SFG and helicopters of the 160th Special Operations Aviation Regiment, all disguised as soldiers of the 10th Mountain Division, arrived on the same base. The Uzbek government had authorized its use, except for offensive actions. In order to launch operations in spite of that political restriction, the teams left from another airstrip, far removed from any human presence and only a few kilometres away from the border. A week later, the Defence Secretary, Donald Rumsfeld, managed to erase all those problems and the Uzbeks offered the use of three new airstrips to the American. The teams were then ready to enter Taliban country.

On October 30, 2001, a meeting of paramount importance was held in Dushanbe, Tadjikistan, between General Tommy Franks, CENTCOM Commander and the main leaders of the anti-Taliban Alliance . The representative of the Pentagon basically told them that America was ready to put all its military weight into the war, provided that its interlocutors could stop their endless squabbles and really decided to join forces with the USA in the anti-Taliban operations.

have to organize units in relation to the air supports of the USAF, the whole process being undertaken in enemy territory and without speaking the local language. The teams were spread on three major fronts: Shomali / Kabul, Samangan / Mazar-e-Sharif and Takhar. Meanwhile, the American secret services convinced (probably by bribery) the famous Uzbek war lord, Abdul Rashid Dostom, to leave his exile in Turkey in order to breath a new lease of life into the dispirited fighters located around the of Darrah-e-Suf resistance pocket, South of Mazar-e-Sharif, his former fiefdom.

On the same day, October 19, a team of Green Berets arrived at Dostom's HQ in Darrah-e-Suf, in order to coordinate American help, to try and organize the first "armoured columns" and to identify commanders capable of assisting the Americans on the front. Discreetly, some CIA Special Operations Group (SOG) operators who had preceded the SF team and who had " prepared the ground " left the area and returned to Uzbekistan in helicopter.

" Need of action " for the media

Pressurized by public opinion, Washington was "in need of some action " because the two operations in the South of the country led by Rangers and Delta Force were not considered as sufficient; orders were given to the American special forces to intensify their efforts and to launch operations in the direction of Mazar-e-Sharif. The purpose of those operations was to seize two airports, both civil and military, in the northern region. However to seize Mazar-e-Sharif, the Coalition could not count on more than 6 000 fighters, with few heavy weapons, no armour and

De Oppresso Liber* on the roads to victory

A NEW WAR FOR THE GREEN BERETS

The definition of Special Forces

The Americans draw a precise line between the Special Forces (SF), which are mostly made up of "Green Berets", and the Special Operations Forces (SOF), within which the Green Berets are integrated but which also include a sizeable number of other "special forces" type of units. In fact, the definition of SOF covers units that are organized, trained, equipped and used only as a specific supplement to conventional forces, in order to reach military, political, economical or psychological goals that tend to be mostly of a strategic nature. These goals are reached through the use of non-conventional means, generally in a hostile or politically sensitive environment.

Three major fronts

From October 19, an unspecified number of green berets teams, like Teams 553, 555 , 585 and 595 (or ODA 553 for Operational Detachment-Alpha 553), were in place; they had already designated targets for several aerial bombardment and they had started training Afghan fighters in order to operate alongside them. Having been helicoptered in, they then had to walk for more than ten hours, carrying their 50 kilos rucksacks. However, from October 30, the number of teams helicoptered into Afghanistan was doubled. The mission seems at first impossible, because the green berets have to win the confidence of the Afghan fighters, then judge the commanders and their capabilities; they then

almost no artillery. Fortunately, if the Taliban could count on roughly the same number of gunmen, they were very thin on the ground and scattered in a region which was openly hostile to them. To arm and equip the Uzbek fighters, the heavy lift aircrafts of the AFSOC parachuted in just a few days dozens of tons of weapons, ammunition, equipment, and even saddles for the American teams which were at the time horse mobile !

From October 21, the different teams began to "paint" enemy targets on the front line with their lasers in order to guide US attack aircrafts. At first, the attacks were undertaken mostly on the north front, then moved on to the Kabul area — previously, air raids had only concentrated on the military infrastructure of the Taliban. However, the leaders of the Alliance were frus-

Above.
A Green beret from the 3rd Special Forces Group checking an "Al-Qaida" weapons cave, Southeast of Afghanistan.
(DOD picture)

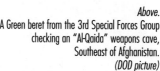

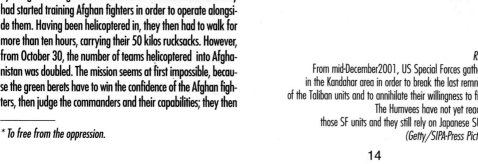

Right.
From mid-December2001, US Special Forces gathered in the Kandahar area in order to break the last remnants of the Taliban units and to annihilate their willingness to fight. The Humvees have not yet reached those SF units and they still rely on Japanese SUVs.
(Getty/SIPA-Press Picture)

* To free from the oppression.

trated by the low intensity of those bombardments. Indeed, in front of the Bagram tracks, one counts only two to four attack aircrafts a day. This was nothing like the desired massive bombardments! It is the time of uncertainty in the ranks of the anti-Taliban groups, because the different factions realize it is now impossible to rely on the " American card " to govern the country after the Taliban regime, namely Abdul Haq the Pachtoun leader. Infiltrated in Afghan territory by a CIA helicopter with some of his people to try to turn the tribes of the East of the country, he was arrested and executed. Very discreetly, taking advantage of the Ranger's airborne and heliborne operations in the South of Afghanistan, a team of green berets belonging to the ODA 574, callsign Texas One-Two, was helicoptered at the same time in the village of Kotwal, near Siskin Kot (in the South of Kandahar), with an important stock of arms, various military equipment and food, but especially with a " major asset", Hamid Karzaï, the future Afghan government chief. On December 4, 2001, thirty kilometres North of Kandahar, he was appointed provisional president. Victory was within reach, at least in the North and in Kabul, and the Green Berets continued "to paint" targets for aviation with their lasers, in particular a convoy of 500 Taliban and a hundred vehicles, destroyed on November 16 in daylight attacks by F-14 and F-18, called in by Texas-One-Two." *We were one against fifty! It was impressive to see this column bristling with weapons arriving toward us!* reported one of the ODA 574 members. *Sergeant Petithory* (who was later KIA) *was behind his tactical laser designator and he used his radio to designate the targets. In just a few minutes, B-52 released their one-ton bombs on the taliban's vehicles. Three hundred talibans were killed and thirty five vehicles destroyed. Nevertheless, they tried to attack again during several days; every time, we called the Air Force. And it was a slaughter! "*

On December 5, B-52s began to bombard a Taliban position

Left.
A joint Special Forces and USAF CCT team on the front line facing Taliban during the last week of October 2001.
(USSOCOM Photo)

Previous page bottom.
On the 26 of November 2001, US Special Forces, Delta Force, British SAS and SBS have just de-bussed from their vehicles in order to stifle the Taliban uprising in the Qala-i-Jangi fortress. At that moment, the second CIA Field Agent has already escaped the enemy gunmen and he is coordinating the action of the Coalition's special forces.
(Jumbish-i-Mili Picture)

Below.
Around the Qala-e-Jangi fortress, on November 26, 2001, a group of Special Forces, with Delta Force reinforcements, get ready to quell the Taliban riot. The fluorescent "glint" blue flashes pinned to the BDUs allow those operators to be identified by the US attack aircrafts.
(Anja Niedringhaus Picture)

Special Forces A-Team

The A-Team, which is also called an Operational Detachment Alpha, is the basic cell of all of the US Army's Special Forces Groups. An SF company is organized in six A-Teams. Each Team, commanded by a captain, is made up of twelve NCOs and officers. The captain's executive officer is a lieutenant. The non-commissioned officers are specialists in each of the five SF specialities: special operations, weapons, engineer, communications and military intelligence. All A-Team members are Special Forces qualified, each member has got several fields of personal expertise and each team can master several foreign languages between its twelve operators.

The strength of those team lay in their ability to perform missions autonomously or as part of a bigger units; to insert and extract of operational zones by air, land and sea; to be able to undertake operations in hostile territory for a sustained period with a minimum of outside support; to create, organize, train and equip local indigenous forces up to battalion-sized units while remaining capable at all time to perform special operations under the command of a Force Commander.

Alpha Detachments also serve as reservoirs for the Special Forces command that can, if needed, put together a mission-tailored temporary unit.In an SF company one of the six A-Teams is SCUBA trained and another one is HALO/HAHO qualified. These two units are mostly deployed on operations requesting discreet or covert insertions.

The SCUBA divers are equipped with conventional open-circuit or military closed circuit Drägger LAR-V breathing apparatus, semi-rigid Zodiacs and Klepper kayaks.

Generally, A-Team are trained and lavishly equipped in order to be autonomous for long periods of time if necessary. This explains why they are equipped with their own communication suites, (satellite, VHF and HF radios), night-vision goggles, GPS, digital cameras, demolition equipments and charges, medical kits including dental instruments, biologic diagnosis kits, sterilizer, resuscitation equipments, water quality control equipments and even veterinarian instruments.

WITH ODA 555 AGAINST THE TALIBANS

Two MH-53J Pave Low helicopter fly at full throttle, nap-of-the-earth in pitch darkness, in a remote Panshir valley. The noise is deafening and inside the helicopter crammed full of men and equipment nobody speaks. The slightest error from the crew and the huge machine and its human cargo would be history." Higher, higher! " Somebody has shouted in the microphone, and the first helicopter of the Air Forces Special Operations Command rises heavily over a mountain that looks even darker than the others, immediately followed by his wingman.

Aboard the two helicopters are twelve men of Team 555 which will have the honour of penetrating ahead of all other SF units into Afghanistan. Twice already, this A-Team of the 5th SFG had to cancel this mission because the weather was too severe between Tadjikistan and the Panshir valley, fief of the Tajik fighters of "major" Massoud, who had died a few weeks before. But, this time, everything seems to be going according to plan. A dull thud. The MH-53 lands in a cloud of dust just after midnight, on October 19, 2001. Not a single light around and, of course (as happens in war films), this is not the right LZ. The two helos have landed on the wrong side of the hill. Each of the green berets has more than 150 kilos of equipment, it is just not feasible to ask them to do a quick reconnaissance of the area.

The team leader, a Chief Warrant Officer, looks sceptical. On the other side of the hill, little lamps seem to be dancing in the wind." *We are in a bad position, he thinks, our night-vision goggles are of no use now. And this is not the reception party I was expecting.* " " *OK lads, if I dive to the ground, you fire at everything that moves; understand?*" And the Chief Warrant Officer, his M4 assault rifle in hand, leaves in the direction of the lights which are now moving towards him, .

Then everything goes very fast; Diaz is suddenly faced with a giant who, (like in a film) crushes his hand in a robust handshake and, with a very strong American accent utters: "*Fuck! You are finally there. I am so pleased to see you!*" The giant is in fact the CIA agent who arrived at the beginning of October, with orders, equipment and a lot of money, which is to be used to facilitate the work of US special forces with the Tajiks of the Alliance.

Team 555 (nicknamed Triple Nickel) is commanded by CWO DIAZ who knows the region well. Indeed, he has already spent seven months on the Pakistan border with Afghanistan in 1987, during a CIA mission, whereas the other members of the team have already been in action in Iraq and in Somalia, and have trained special forces in the Middle East.

The CIA team immediately guides the SF team towards a "*safe house*" where the agents give a quick situation update and brief the newcomers on the mission at hand: " *Tomorrow, you will meet general Fahim, Defence Minister of the Alliance, and one of us will present you to generals Babajan and Bismullah Khan.*"

On the next day, at 7 o'clock, near Bagram, Bismullah Khan seems very suspicious when faced with those extremly well equiped soldiers. "*Show us what you can do* ", says Bismullah Khan. The four team members observe the Taliban positions.They are spoilt for choice: for two weeks the local front has been strengthened and there are now 7 000 talibans and more than fifty targets, tanks, armored cars, artillery pieces, headquarters and bunkers.

Quickly, Diaz sets up his tactical laser designator (TLD) and transmits with the help of an Air Force CCT. Everybody settles down in the destroyed control tower of the Bagram airport, the best seats around. "*General, can you see the antennae which are visible on top of this hill?*" At the same time, an F / A-18 Hornet from the USS THEODORE ROOSEVELT passes overhead. The aircraft is guided on his bombing run and destroys the target with a plume of smoke. It is a complete success with the Afghans who applaud. CWO Diaz even receives a kiss from the Afghan general! The staff of the Alliance then provides the SF operators with an endless list of targets to destroy and the team remains on site for more than seven hours until the last aircrafts disappears towards the Indian Ocean.

While Team 555 tries to destroy everything in front of Bagram, three supplementary Teams entered Afghanistan: Team 553, in the central province of Bamian; Team 585, not far from Kunduz; and T eam 595, to Darrah-e-Suf, in the new headquarters of the famous Abdul Rashid Dostom.

On November 12, having well and truly crushed the Taliban defences , the restless Tajik units began their advance towards Kabul. The Green Berets witness the surrendering of Taliban before penetrating into the city at the same time as general Fahim, who, for the occasion, had put on his brand new chinese battle dress. Finally Team 555 was the first to enter the US embassy which had been closed since 1989. Mission accomplished.

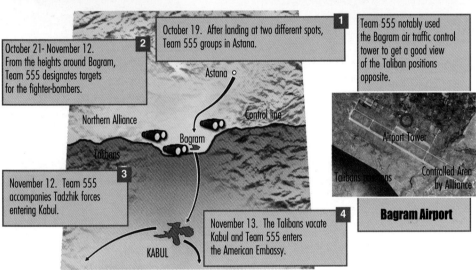

October 19. After landing at two different spots, Team 555 groups in Astana.

October 21- November 12. From the heights around Bagram, Team 555 designates targets for the fighter-bombers.

Team 555 notably used the Bagram air traffic control tower to get a good view of the Taliban positions opposite.

November 12. Team 555 accompanies Tadzhik forces entering Kabul.

November 13. The Talibans vacate Kabul and Team 555 enters the American Embassy.

Northern Alliance

Talibans

Astana

Control line

Bagram

KABUL

Airport Tower

Talibans positions

Controlled Area by Allliance

Bagram Airport

Above. Elements of Team 555 in position in Bagram's airport control tower guiding American aircraft on Taliban targets.

Left. From a position overlooking the plain of Shomali, Green Berets observe Taliban movements a few days before they started retreating.

Below left. An ODA 555 team member inside a Safe House with his communication equipments.

Below right. A Green Beret belonging to ODA 555 tracking a target and giving coordinates to one of his teammates who will be doing the final guidance of a laser guided weapon. *(USSOCOM Pictures)*

In the vicinity of Kandahar, in the South of Afghanistan, acting on specific information, US Special Forces operators lead a joint patrol with local guides in order to locate and intercept Taliban groups before they enter the villages of the area.
(AP/SIPA-Press Picture)

that was very close to the SF operators when a bomb fell less than fifty metres from the special forces group. Three Americans and ten Afghans were instantly killed, and forty others were wounded, including the new President. ODA 574 had been dealt a very severe blow and had to return to the USA.

Kandahar fell on December 7

At this moment, it is possible to identify at least ten different green berets teams, the famous A-Teams made up of thir-

Green Beret soldier on a reconnaissance mission in a section of Kabul.
For this mission, he is wearing the polar fleece issued to the USSOCOM units, civilian-made tactical pants, and the Afghan pakôl and scarf used by the Special Forces operating with the mudjahidin of the Northern Alliance. He has an HK USP pistol, and note the Microtech automatic folding knife in one of the straps of his Eagle MkV holster.

Member of the 5th Special Forces on operation in Kandahar, getting ready to jump into a 4x4 with his teammates. He is wearing a SPEAR/USSOCOM polar fleece, a "commando" woolen bonnet, "tactical" gloves and Oakley M-Frame military balistics goggles. His weapons include the traditional Colt M-16 A2 (M-4) equiped with an Airpoint sight and a Beretta 92 PA in a Safariland SLS holster.

THE US ARMY SPECIAL FORCES COMMAND (Airborne)

On November 27, 1990, the US Army's 1st Special Operations Command became the US Army Special Forces Command (Airborne). The principal missions of this command are to train, test and prepare the Army's special units in order to insure that they are ready to be deployed around the world for the benefit of the various US commands.

THE USASFC (A) has a total of five active and two National Guard units (called Groups) under its command. Each group is made up of three battalions, a support company and a command company. Every battalion has six detachments called Operational Detachment Alpha or ODA (also called A-Team) under its command. Unlike other Division-sized units, USASFC (A) is not located in one single base; it is divided between the East and West coasts and on numerous other bases around the world.

The Special Forces missions - unique within the American armed forces because they can equally be carried out in peacetime, during crisis and in the course of a high intensity war - are: unconventional warfare, Foreign Internal Defence, deep reconnaissance, direct offensive actions and counter-terrorism. The "Green Berets'" major mission consists in working with countries linked with the USA to form, train and help in any which way possible their armed and police forces. Very often, Special Forces get involved in other units' missions: support of local units engaged in military actions, Combat Search And Rescue (CSAR), assistance to the internal security services, peacekeeping, humanitarian relief, antiterrorism and anti-narcotics operations.

ce NCOs, as well as one or two Delta operators or CIA agents. They almost all belong to the 1st , 2nd , 3rd and 5th, as well as to the HHC of the 5th SFG. CENTCOM had allocated a strengthened Team to each of the Alliance's leaders. All together, a total of three hundred and sixteen Army Special Forces members, or eighteen A-Teams, four company command cells and three battalion command cells.

Horses against 4 x 4 vehicles

It is necessary to remember that the first offensive launched between the 17th and the 20th of October in the Akkupruq zone failed and that the Taliban managed to recapture all the lost ground. But in the space of a week, everything changed, with the help of the Special Forces teams; and the troops of the four factions of the Alliance, Dostom's Uzbeks, the Jamiat people under "major" Atta, the Shiites of Hizbi-i-Wahdat and those of Hussein Anwari's Harakat-i-Islami, who had decided to stop arguing and to coordinate their efforts. On November 3, Lieutenant-Colonel Max Bowers, commanding officer of the 5th Group, and his new forces link up with Dostom's HQ andTeam 595. Their mission is to coordinate the various attacks of the commanders of the North. On November 4, the second offensive is a complete success! Kashendeh-ye Bala and Akkupruq are taken, the gorges of Sholgarah fall the next day, and on November 9, at 1900, the first elements enter Mazar-e-Sharif. The green berets teams find it difficult to follow the pace of the advance because they constantly have to set up and dismantle their TLDs and radios to remain among the troops in contact and provide them with tactical air support. This time, they had to leave their horses behind and exchange them for much faster Japanese 4X4 vehicles.

To explain the series of defeats suffered by the talibans in front of Mazar-e-Sharif, it is necessary to know that they had not prepared any secondary lines of defence and that the majority of

their heavy armament was stored in Mazar-e-Sharif. All this armament was then abandoned when they ran away towards Kunduz in the East, the only zone where the Pachtoune minority was favorable to them. Then followed a moment of uncertainty for the teams, because in spite of the "domino"effect which sees cities falling one after the other, they have to stay on their guard, knowing there are still uncontrolled elements at large. But it is unmistakably a big success, every team having achieved impressive "scores" , team Tiger 03 for example being credited with the destruction of 1 300 Taliban, 50 tanks, armored vehicles, artillery pieces and bunkers.

Before and after Tora Bora

After the fall of Mazar-e-Sharif, Teams of Army Special Forces, with Air Force Combat Control Team and Pararescuemen, launched several rapid reconnaissance missions on the two airports in order to assess the damage they have suffered and to allow the swift arrival of Air Force aircrafts. Some hours later, the first AFSOC and CIA helicopters land at the end of the runway, disgorging CIA SOG operators clad in in a mix of western and traditional afghan garb. With the seizure of the border city of Heiratan which faces Uzbekistan and which made the arrival by road of special forces vehicles possible,the SF no longer needed to be brought in by helicopter as before . From November 11, the strategists of the Pentagon "tip over" the front and intensify aerial bombardments in front of Bagram. From then on, the Special Forces teams can go into full action, designating dozens of targets that are then subsequently engaged by the coalition's attack aircraft as well as by B52 and B1B heavy bombers. The Taliban lines of defence collapse and, on November 12, the Taliban leave Kabul during the night. Surprised by this move, the Americans launch several CIA and green berets teams on a clandestine mission that is not normally devolved to an Army unit which is basically to recover as many documents on " Al-Qaida "

Above, left.
Even five days after its fall, Kandahar still was considered a very dangerous city for foreigners. In order to protect pro-American Afghan dignitaries and American envoys to the country, joint Special Forces/Delta close protection details were activated until the city became safer. *(Getty/SIPA-Press Picture)*

Above right.
A 5th SFG Green Beret taking pictures with a digital camera before sending them via satellite to his command in Florida.
(USSOCOM Picture)

Right.
On the 25th of May 2002, a 5th SFG operator delivers UNICEF-provided humanitarian relief to a school near Kabul. Apart from strictly military operations, the US Special Forces have always included CIMIC (Civil-Military Cooperation) among their missions. *(USAF Picture)*

as possible before crowds scatters or burns them.

The teams operating in the North of the country stayed in their zones because the resistance pockets of Taliban and Arab volunteers were still important, especially around Kunduz (which finally fell on November 26, 2001, after severe fighting and especially intense bombardment guided by Special Forces operators). At the same time, those of the "Centre" and the "South" (about which little is known) penetrated in Afghanistan trough Pakistan and headed for Kandahar and Ghazny. The airport here was to serve as an advanced base for all American Special Forces and a part of British special forces. While this was happening, on November 15, a joint SAS/SBS detachment seized Bagram air base, to the utmost annoyance of the local Alliance leaders who had not been pre warned of that move.

If certain elements of the green berets were then allowed a bit of slack, from November 25 those in the North were called in to subdue and then destroy the revolt of the Qala-e-Jangi prison (see page 32).

During Operation *Anaconda* in March 2002, in front of a row of CH-47F Chinook helicopters, an SF team gets ready to board a chopper with a 101st Air Assault Division squad. Note that a certain leeway in the dress code was still tolerated at that point in the campaign. *(DOD Picture)*

eft.
2 In January 2002, in the Gardez area, southeast of Afghanistan, Green Berets" patrol in an up-armoured Humvee. At that period, liban were still active in that area.
Getty / SIPA-Press Picture)

Right.
While Northern Alliance units were already starting to deploy in the area after the fall of Kandahar, US Special Forces were still very much in evidence in the city. This SF operator belongs to the teams which deployed to Afghanistan from Pakistan in mid-November 2001. He wears the traditional Afghan hat, the Pakol, and he carries his rifle magazines in a Chinese "Chicom" chest webbing.
(AP/SIPA-Press Picture)

Bottom, from left to right.
Several "Green Berets" of the 1st Battalion, 3rd Special Forces Group, ne of whom is on a Quad motorcycle, doing the recce of a tunnel dug as an air raid shelter by Taliban in the mountain close to Kabul.
(USAF Picture)

United Special Operations Command (USSOCOM)

It is on April 16, 1987 that USSOCOM was officially created as a unified combatant command. Situated on MacDill AFB in Florida, and commanded by a lieutenant general with the title of Commander-in-Chief United States Special Operations Command (USCINCSOC) it has under its orders all the Army, Navy and Air Force SOF. All SOF of the Army, Navy, and Air Force based in the United States are placed under USCINCSOC's combatant command. USSOCOM has three service component commands: Army Special Operations Command (USASOC) Ft. Bragg, NC; Naval Special Warfare Command (NAVSPECWARCOM) Coronado, CA; Air Force Special Operations Command (AFSOC) Hurlburt Field, FL; and one sub-unified command, Joint Special Operations Command (JSOC) that was created in 1980 in Ft. Bragg, NC.

USSOCOM exists to provide special operations forces to the National Command Authority (NCA), regional combatant commanders, and American ambassadors and their country teams for successful conduct of special operations during both peace and war. USSOCOM prepares SOF to successfully conduct special operations, including civil affairs and psychological operations.

The responsibilities of USSOCOM are quite numerous and they include: Insuring the readiness of assigned forces and monitoring the readiness of overseas SOF, monitoring the professional development of all SOF personnel, developing joint SOF tactics, techniques, and procedures, conducting specialized courses of instruction, training assigned forces, executing its own program and budget (its funding comes directly from Congress and not from the Services) and finally conducting research, development, and acquisition of special operations peculiar items.

Six regional commands

Since 1988 each of the theatre unified commands have established a separate Special Operations Command (SOC) to meet its theatre-unique special operations requirements. Those commands are: Special Operations Command Atlantic Command (SOCACOM) in Norfolk (USA), Special Operations Command Central (SOCCENT) in MacDill (USA), Special Operations Command Europe (SOCEUR) in Vaihinger (Germany), Special Operations Command Pacific (SOCPAC) in Camp Smith (Hawaii), Special Operations Command Korea (SOCKOR) in Yonson (Korea), Special Operations Command South (SOCSOUTH) in Miami (USA).

No fixed organization, but an organized force

During operations, three types of Special Operations Force Joint Task Force or JTF can be formed under the command of the Joint Forces Commander. These commands are the Joint Special Operations Task Force (JSOTF), the Joint Psychological Operations Task Force (JPOTF) and the Joint Civil Military Operations Task Force (JCMOTF). These units are created according to the operation, and have variable composition and "life expectancies".

A Joint Special Operations Task Force has no fixed, rigid organization. The size of its HQ varies from less than twenty to over two hundred depending on the mission. It is organized as a conventional Task Force, including representatives from the three services detached from the regional Special Forces command; it is always possible to tailor the staff to the mission, reinforcing it if necessary with elements seconded from other regions. The mission of the JSOTF consists in undertaking special operations in association with other commands on the ground and in formulating recommendations or criticisms on the use of Special Forces by the overall commander.

A Joint Psychological Operations Task Force is made up of psychological operations units leading psychological actions in support of other units. According to the actions, the unit's size is naturally very variable, and the JSOTF commander can sometimes only need a single PSYOPS team. Most of the time, a Special Forces commander will place one or several PSYOPS teams within special units. The JPOTF missions are many folds; advising the JTF commander on psychological actions, elaborating situation reports or participating in concerted actions with allied units to name but a few. The PSYOPS' missions are to disseminate information and messages to foreign audiences in order to influence their feelings, their motives, their opinions and reactions toward politicians, organizations, groups, people or even whole countries. Quite simply, psychological operations aim to influence the mentalities of foreign populations to have them support american objectives. To reach those goals, one of the main tools in the hands of the PSYOPS teams remains the USAFSOC EC-130E Solo Commando. In the field, PSYOPS team works at corps, division and brigade levels.

Coordinating the actions of SOFs and conventional units.

To insure the best possible coordination with conventional units, US Special Forces can count on a number of joint coordination teams. Special Operations Coordination Element (SOCOORD) works at Army corps Marine Expeditionary Force (MEF) level; its mission is to integrate the special units into the organization and operations plans; one level down, Special Operations Command and Control Element (SOCCE) are very often set up within the Special Forces' command company of the Army's "B-Teams" (SFOD-B) or within Ranger units as liaison element. One can also find several SOCCE within an armed force or of a MEF under the command of the Joint Forces Special Operations Component Commander (JFSOCC). In more ways than one, the SOCCE is a vital element of ground and maritime operations coordination. The SPECIAL OPERATIONS LIAISON ELEMENT (SOLE) is made up of USAFSOC liaison officers whose mission is to deal with all matters relevant to the USAF within a special operation framework. "Deconfliction" is very often the name of the game for those officers who always have to make sure the SOFs and the USAF work together and not inadvertently one against the other. SOLE are directly under JFSOCC command.

Finally, the Naval Special Warfare Task Unit (NSWTU) is a temporarily subordinated unit within the Naval Special Warfare Group (NSWTG) that is tasked with the command, the control, the administrative coordination, the logistic support and the integration of special operations within maritime operations. It is also noteworthy that Naval Special Warfare (NSW) Forces often operate under a conventional naval command.

An SF close protection team operating from a civilian 4 x 4 vehicle in support of Afghan authorities in the former Taliban stronghold of Kandahar, December 12, 2001.
(Getty/SIPA-Press Picture)

Three weeks later, the American special forces tactical command had to round up most of the available teams to intervene in the Tora Bora region (see boxed text). The limited success of this operation led the Americans to take the complete situation in their own hands and to leave very little leeway to the Afghan forces. Some days earlier, on January 4, Sergeant First Class Nathan Chapman of the 3rd Bn. (ODA 194) of the 1st SFG based in Fort Lewis had been killed during a firefight not far from Gardez. He was the first green beret to be KIA in Afghanistan.

At the end of January and the beginning of February, 2002, the first teams who had been deployed as early as October 2001 are sent back to the USA. They are relieved in place by elements belonging to the Special Forces, Psyops units, Civilian Affairs units and crews belonging to the 160th SOAR. Those elements took part in all the operations, the purely American one as well as the Coalition ones; they worked in particular with the 82nd and the 101st Divisions.

On March 3, Army Chief Warrant Officer Stanley L. Harriman of the 3rd Bn. of the 3rd SFG is killed by a mortar shell during *Operation Anaconda*. Several teams of US special forces including a mix of seven SEAL operators and green berets, each team being in control of about fifty Afghan soldiers, received the mission of blocking the passes between Gardez and Khost. The Americans, who had by then understood the tactics of the Talibans after studying them in Tora Bora, decided to establish observation posts on the trails leading into neighbouring Pakistan. However, the US staff at Bagram subsequently acknowledged the fact that such a mission was impossible to pull off: " *To think that we could totally surround a 150 km2 mountainous zone was nothing but an illusion. So, it is very unlikely that we will catch Taliban fighters in our net and that we will see them carrying their dead comrades into the plain below*".

On April 15, Sergeant First Class Daniel Romero of the Colorado National Guard Army Special Force is killed with three other soldiers when a 107 mm rocket that was being destroyed exploded near Kandahar. From the middle of May 2002, elements of the 1st Battalion of the 3rd SFG is tasked with a new mission: the formation of four battalions of the future Afghan army. These green berets of the 1st Bn. are specialists in this type of training: since 1996, they had already trained a number of foreign units, especially in Africa.

In May, 2002, the green berets are regrouped and Khost becomes their main operating base. Other US special forces as well as coalition SF also operate from Khost. Most of the search operations that are regularly launched against Taliban and "Al-Qaida" gunmen that are still hiding in the mountains that mark the border with Pakistan originate from this city. On May 19, Army Natio-

The US Army Special Forces

The US ARMY SPECIAL OPERATIONS FORCES (ARSOF) are made up of over 26 000 soldiers belonging to active duty or Army Reserve and National Guard units. These forces are centred on Special Forces units, Rangers' units, Air Force special operations units, Civil Affairs units, Psychological Operations units and special operations support units. ARSOF headquarters, as well as the John-F.-Kennedy Special Warfare Centre and the Special Forces schools are all located in Fort Bragg, North Carolina.

A total of five active duty Special Operations Groups (Airborne) are currently located in Fort Bragg, Fort Lewis, Fort Campbell and Fort Carson, as well as two other National Guard Special Forces Groups based in Alabama and in Utah. The elite 75th Ranger Regiment is garrisoned in Fort Benning.

The 160th Special Operations Aviation Regiment (Airborne), the Special Force's Aviation unit, is located in Fort Campbell. Its current inventory includes MH-47E, MH-60L and MH-6M helicopters, crewed by hand picked pilots who are all capable of flying equally effectively by day or night and in the most difficult environments.

The Army special units that are currently the most often deployed across the world are the Civil Affairs; they belong to the 96th Civil Affairs Battalion (Airborne), an active duty unit, as well as to four Army Reserve units, located in Florida, California, Maryland and New York.

The Psychological Operations Units are tasked with the dissemination of information to very wide audiences by the unlimited use of all sorts of media, radio, television, Internet, free publications and public meetings all aimed directly at the theatre of operations. The 4th Psychological Operations Group (Airborne) is located in Fort Bragg, and the two Army Reserve units are in Ohio and California.

Finally, Fort Bragg is also the main camp of the various support and special missions units, among which the most famous is the 1st Special Forces Operational Detachment-Delta, often called Delta Force. This unit, recently deployed to Afghanistan and to the Philippines, receives extremely thorough training in many fields but specializes in antiterrorist operations and hostage rescue.

From top to bottom.
Those pictures depict the arrival on the 14th of May 2002 of new Afghan army recruits. Several hundred of those recruits were to follow a 10-week training syllabus devised and taught by 150 US SF operators in order to make up the new platoons, companies and battalions of the reformed Afghan Army. Here, the new recruits are given their uniforms and field gear. *(DOD Picture)*

Previous pages.
Special Forces Humvees driving across a ruined part of the city of Kabul in December 2002. From the end of winter 2002, the Japanese SUVs were systematically replaced by armoured Humvees. The civilian 4X4s were from then on only used as liaison vehicles or for covert operations. *(Christophe Roussel Picture)*

Location and Geographical areas of responsibilities of the Special Forces Groups

1st Special Forces Group (Airborne), based in Fort Lewis in the State of Washington, also has a battalion in Okinawa in Japan. It is under USPACOM command.

3rd Special Forces Group (Airborne), based in Fort Bragg, North Carolina, has Africa as its area of responsibility. It is under USEUCOM command.

5th Special Forces Group (Airborne), based in Fort Campbell, Kentucky, is under CENTCOM command.

7th Special Forces Group (Airborne), based in Fort Bragg, North Carolina, also has a company in Porto Rico. It is under SOUTHCOM command.

10th Special Forces Group (Airborne), based in Fort Carson, Colorado, also has a battalion in Stuttgart, Germany. It is under USEUCOM command.

19th Special Forces Group (Airborne), based in Salt Lake City, Utah, is under USPACOM command.

20th Special Forces Group (Airborne) is based in Birmingham, Alabama. It is under SOUTHCOM command.

Right.
Beginning of a patrol for US Special Forces operators in the Khost region during the summer of 2002. They are about to patrol a yet-to-be-secured area where the presence of Afghan Army and Coalition units has not managed to completely remove the Taliban and "Al Qaida" threat which still trickles in Afghanistan from the infamous Pakistani "Tribal areas". The beard and the complete lack of uniform discipline will probably remain one of the long lasting memories of the US SF involvement in Afghanistan. *(AP/SIPA-Press Picture)*

Green berets rewarded for heroism

On January 15, 2001, in Fort Campbell, the Army Chief of Staff, general Eric Shinseki, rewarded nineteen green berets for heroism in Afghanistan. During the ceremony, twelve Green Berets of Headquarters and Headquarters Company, and 2nd and 3rd Battalions of the 5th SFG (A) received Bronze Stars: Capt. Kevin C. Leahy, Capt. Paul R. Syverson, Capt. Jason Amerine, Sgt. 1st Class Michael McElhiney Jr. Sgt Gilbert Magallenes Jr. Sgt. 1st Class Ronnie Raikes, Staff Sgt. Bradley Fowers, Sgt. 1st Class Vaughn Berntson, Staff Sgt. Wesley McGirr, Sgt. 1st Class Christopher Pickett, 1st Sgt. David B. Betz, Sgt. 1st Class Paul Beck. It is noteworthy that four of them received Bronze Stars with V for valour in action.

Eight of those operators had, in December, 2001, received the Purple Heart, at the same time as Capt. John Leopold, Chief Warrant Officer 2 Terry Reed, Staff Sgt. Hamid Fathi of the 2nd Bn. / 5th SFG (A) and Sgt. 1st Class David Kennedy of the 2nd Bn. / 5th SFG (A).

The Chief of Staff of the American armies, general Eric K . Shinseki, decorating captain Jason L. Amerine of the 5th Special Forces Group with the Bronze Star with V for heroic action in Afghanistan.
(US Army Picture)

American Special Forces aboard a civilian 4 x 4 Toyota Hilux SUV in the southeast of Afghanistan in February 2002. From the first days of November the American special forces bought a fleet of civilian 4 x 4 vehicles like this one; those vehicles could be armed in this instance with an M240B 7,62mm machine gun fitted with a Litton light intensifying scope turning them into very efficient and cost effective general purpose "Technicals" for the SF operators.
(Getty / SIPA-Press Picture)

nal Guard Special Force Sergeant Gene Arden Vance, 19th SFG of the National Guard of the Virginia, dies in an ambush in the east of Afghanistan. In response, Special Forces units launched a raid in the zone where Vance was killed, in parallel with Royal Marine units that were then searching the mountains in the North as part of *Operation Condor*.

On June 17, 2002, a special forces patrol comes under fire at 11. 30, near the city of Siskin Kot, North of Kandahar. The US Special Forces shot and killed two gunmen who had opened up on them. At the same moment, on the border with Pakistan, another mixed US special forces and Afghan patrol takes fire from light weapons in an ambush set up near the village of Dhkin. Immediately, the Americans called in an AC-130 which leveled the houses from which the shots had emanated.Ten days later, in the province of Konar, US Green Berets come under mortar fire and request tactical air support; an F-18 dropped two 500 lbs bombs on the supposed Taliban position. The attackers having already made for the border, the aerial attack had no effective result.

On July 12, the US special forces camp near Siskin Kot, in the province of Oruzgan, is attacked at night with

US Special Forces providing close protection to General Dostom. The Green Beret were very numerous among Northern Alliance units. A few of them, wearing civilian clothes, were tasked with the close protection of famous

General Rachid Dostom. There is nothing military about their appearance; denim trousers and shirts and New York Fire Department baseball caps. The HF radio complete with ear piece and throat mike and the Glock 17 pistol and Colt M-4 rifle are all parts of the normal "BG" (Body Guard) tools.

At the conclusion of military operations in the North of Afghanistan, the commander of American Special Forces visited the still deployed units and congratulated them for their successes.
(USSOCOM Picture)

grenades and automatic weapons. Nevertheless, at end of July, the talibans and "Al-Qaida" threat is still present in the southeast of Afghanistan. The fighters of these two movements being always able to find assistance amongst the Pachtoune population of these regions, which opposes the multiethnic government of Kabul. It is necessary to keep in mind that the majority of " Al-Qaida" training camps were situated in this zone which borders Pakistan. Moreover, at the beginning of August, a Yemenite is arrested in the Karghi district with three antitank missiles. Five days later, a group of US Special Forces, operating alongside an 82nd Airborne division unit made a night arrest,near Khost, of three suspected " Al-Qaida "members. " The war on several fronts" of October and November, 2001 is now only a distant memory for the green berets of the USSOCOM, who now continue their searches and their collection of information. Just another type of mission for those specialists of unconventional warfare.

On this warm and sunny Saturday of November the 24th 2001 about three hundred Taliban, Pakistani and Arabic volunteers who had just fled the bombardments of the Kunduz pocket in the North of Afghanistan decided to hand in their weapons about ten kilometres from Mazar-e-Sharif. They surrendered to general Abdul Rashid Dostom, who immediately claimed to have achieved a brilliant victory. The prisoners were embarked on lorries, and taken to the Qala-e-Jangi fortress that is located close to Mazar-e-Sharif.

Although Dostom is renowned to be very hard on his enemies-even according to the Afghan warlords criteria!- this time he had decided to try a different, more lenient approach by quickly releasing the Taliban so that they could return home. The foreign Islamist volunteers were, on the other hand, handed in to the UN. Dostom's men committed the first of many errors when they did not properly search their prisoners before escorting them towards their prison, the XIXth century Qala-e-Jangi, fortress which Dostom also used as a stable for his cavalry and as an ammunition dump.

Once the Taliban arrive at the prison, events quickly turned sour. As they enter the prison, they were ordered to empty their pockets; A prisoner waited for Nadir Ali, one of the main commanders of the Alliance to walk past him to produce a hand grenade and to blow Nadir and himself up. A few hours later, after the sun has set, another prisoner managed to kill another Hazaras commander, Said Asad. One has to remember that most of those six hundred prisoners arrested during the fall of Mazar-e-Sharif on November 9 had not been searched. In front of those attacks, the guards then decided to push all the prisoners inside the various tunnels that crisscross the underground of the fort under the " pink house " in the centre and in the southernmost courtyard of the fortress. Paradoxically, in spite of those suicide attacks, the guard contingent of the prison was not strengthened.

Two very special Americans

The following morning, on Sunday November 25 hundreds of Alliance soldiers decided to search their prisoners and to oust them from the tunnels under the south yard. At that point, the prisoners enjoyed a certain freedom of movement; they could wash freely and attend to their morning prayers. However, their number in the yard quickly grew, without any armed guards to control them. In this very same yard, two very special Americans, belonging to the CIA, Johnny Michael Spann aged thirty-two and another CIA operator identified as "Dave" were trying to identify in the mass of prisoners "Al-Qaida's" members.

Probably fooled by the peaceful attitude of the Taliban, the two agents decide not to interrogate them individually. This error was going to prove fatal. Spann began by asking a few questions to an individual; the prisoner was quickly joined by another one, then by two others and in a few seconds the CIA operator was surrounded by a crowd of prisoners. Asking one of them: "Why are you here?" The prisoner answered in broken English: "to kill you!", hitting him violently in the neck as he spoke. Spann reached for his pistol and killed him. Dave killed another Taliban, then seized the AK-47 of a guard and shot at the group that surrounded them. According to the witnesses of the scene who were interrogated by a German cameramen team who was then present in the fortress, the prisoners caught Spann,

pushed him to the ground and beat him to death. The CIA man did however manage to kill two of his aggressors, before disappearing in the seething mass. His body was recovered a few days later, completely unrecognisable. CIA agent MICHAEL SPANN thus became the first American to die in Afghanistan during operation Enduring Freedom.

The prisoners then took advantage of the general chaos to seize the weapons of the closest guards and to kill them. At the same time, after having shot three Taliban who were trying to catch him, Dave ran towards the main building which was located along the north outer wall. "Move! The prisoners are coming after me!" he shouted at the two Red Cross representatives who were engaged in a discussion with the prison's "director". " He really was in a state of shock" said a British member of the Red Cross some time later, "and he told us that about twenty guards had died and that the Taliban had taken control of the fortress." While Dave and some guards were trying to save Spann, the Red Cross representatives climbed on top of the walls and jumped on the other side. At the same time, the German TV team, who had been alerted by the gunshots, were running away towards the main building, where it suddenly found itself isolated with Dave by the Taliban fire. The CIA agent, who had lost his satellite telephone in the first confrontation, borrowed the German's phone and managed to reach the American embassy in Tashkent, Uzbekistan. The call was then "transferred" to the US Command telephone exchange in Florida, which immediately tried to contact the special units that were the closest to the fortress. Luckily, a mixed group of British SAS and SBS, American green berets and Delta Forces operators, as well as a company of the 10th Mountain Division was located less than ten kilometres from there. Help was soon under way.

Less than a hundred metres from the place where Dave had taken refuge, the Taliban were releasing their companions from their gaols and some were already trying to escape the fortress using a drain that passes under the south wall. They did not go very far as Northern Alliance soldiers, who had taken up defensive positions around the fortress, brought down a murderous fire upon them. However, inside the fortress, the prisoners had managed to seize one of the arms stockpiles and they soon were distributing AK-47s, RPG-7s, hand grenades, mines, mortars and huge quantities of ammunition. At that point, Northern Alliance forces were still holding all of the southwestern buildings as well as the Northern ramparts and the roof of the main building. Two Northern Alliance tanks even took up position along the north wall and started firing over open sight at the Taliban. But the heaviest fighting took place around the main courtyard.

The "cavalry" arrives!

Sunday November 25, 2001 at around 2PM. Two big 4 x 4 vehicles with tinted windows, followed by a pair of white-painted (in order to look like NGO vehicles) Land Rovers fitted with machine guns on the roof came to a halt in front of the main door of the fortress. Nine Americans special operators debussed, baseball caps on their heads, eyes shielded by Oakley "shades", M-4 assault rifle at the ready. They could be members of the Delta Force, green berets, a mix of Delta Force and CIA. Nobody knows but them! Identifying the six men who jumped out of the white Land Rovers was easier; even dressed in Afghan garbs with big scarves and pakòls, they unmistakably were SAS and SBS. All those highly trained operators had come for two reasons: to save the CIA

Two American Special Forces operators probably belongin to the "Green Berets" observe the Taliban prisoners' movement from the top of the prison's walls. The rapid reactio of American and British special forces broke the back of the revo and made the rescue of some Westerners who were sti trapped in the fortress (including a CIA agent) possible (Getty/SIPA-Press Picture

Righ
The Qala-e-Jangi fortress-cum-jail a few month after the fightings The walls that had been destroyed by american air attacks have alread been rebuilt and all traces of the fierce fights that took plac there removed. During several days, those military operations wer broadcasted on TV as the world watched (ECPAD Picture

THE BATTLE FOR
THE QALA-E-JANGI PRISON

agents and to terminate the revolt. After liaising with the Afghan commander on the ground, the Western SF decided to quickly assault the fortress. The leader of the American group then phoned a mysterious correspondent: "*I want a CCT, a laser designator and precision ammunition. Tell them there is a series of buildings, six or seven, all lined up in the same southeast sector of the fortress. And tell them that if they hit them, they will kill a hell of a lot of those sons of bitches*"

During this time, one of the Americans, a bearded man wearing a splendid Harley-Davidson cap raised Dave, the CIA agent who was still trapped inside the fortress, on the radio: " *Shit!... Hey! man, we are going to get you out of here.*" Then, putting back the mike on the radio set, he turned to another man, another bearded operator who seemed to be the commander of the element. "*Mike has disappeared. The bastards took him and his weapons. Dave managed to escape them so far, but he is surrounded in the northern part of the fortress and he is very low on ammo...*" Then a long discussion followed between those two operators in order to decide which tactics to adopt. Taking up the radio again, the leader of the group then told Dave: "*OK, now we are going to stop those fuckers and when it's done we'll enter the fortress.*" Then, pointing to the sky, he told the Air Force Combat Controller Team who had just arrived with its laser designa-

tors: "*Tell the lads above to stop scratching their asses and to get to work now, we have a job for them!*"

Outside the fortress, the Northern Alliance soldiers began to take position on the walls to try to hold back the Taliban's attacks. The wounded slide down the ramparts and were evacuated in commandeered taxis. Around noon, the battle took a new dimension; the air was thick with bullets. Flying high above the fortress, two American attack aircrafts were waiting for their prey.

On the ground, a meeting with Afghan general Majid Rozi helped to determine what tactics to follow and what were the exact buildings that could now be destroyed by the American aircrafts.

"*Four minutes three minutes two minutes thirty seconds fifteen seconds*"; the countdown of the Air Force CCT who was "painting" his target with a laser beam from his Tactical Laser Designator (TLD) was deadly quiet. At 16.05 exactly, the first GBU-32 JDAM bomb struck one of the fortress's building, causing an enormous explosion. Six other air strikes were going to follow and they literally broke the will of the Taliban to carry out more attacks. After every aerial bombardment, orders were given to the Northern Alliance soldiers to fire with all their weapons, something they did with great gusto but only after having clapped at each and every American bomb attack!

Monday , November 26, 2001. During the night, the exchanges of shots has been uninterrupted. The American and the British Special Forces remained on their positions, taking turns on the ramparts. They occupied three positions: near the main door, under the northeast tower and a last one three hundred metres north outside of the fortress. Taking advantage of the darkness, Dave and the German journalists managed to escape by passing over the north wall. In the morning, Dostom's troops established a new post in the northeast tower, in order to control the mortars and the tank shelling of the Taliban positions. The adjustments given by this observation post are good and the prisoners' resistance begins to weaken. But they still have a good grip on the entire southern half of the fortress on a stretch of two hundred fifty to three hundred metres.

At about 10 o'clock, five supplementary Special Forces operators and ten soldiers of the 10th Mountain Division who form a quick reaction force are in position a few hundred metres outside the fortress. At the same moment, inside the old fort, the CCT got ready to "paint" three more targets. "*Attention, the group which is near the north wall, the pilot of the attack aircraft thinks you are way too close to the target!*" The answer of the group is then heard: "*Yes, it's true, but we have to stay there to paint the target accurately.*" At 10.53, a one-ton GBU-32 laser-guided bomb explodes on the north wall, less than ten metres from the headquarters of the Alliance. Riveted to his binoculars, a US Special Force operator shouts: "*Good God, it is not the right*

place!" A tank is hit, its turret destroyed, and, after a few minutes, the survivors and the wounded begin to emerge from the dust cloud. Within the next twenty minutes, five Americans Special Forces and four British SAS are listed as wounded including a serious wound for a British operator, and another thirty Northern Alliance soldiers are listed as killed and fifty wounded.

The wounded British Special Forces trooper is immediately helicoptered to Uzbekistan, loaded into a cargo plane and flown to a military hospital in Germany.

After a few hours of calm, shots erupted again and, at about 16.50, a Special Forces team returned with Dave. "*This time, we are going to go for it said a Green Beret to an Anglo-Saxon journalist. Stay here tonight and you will not be disappointed!*" Then the Green Beret borrowed the satellite telephone of the journalist and called up his wife in the United States: "*Record all the CNN news Baby!*" At midnight, the show began with two AC-130 "Gunship" which, during five endless gun passes, illuminated the fort with thousands of tracer rounds and grenades, crushing the insurgents under a rain of steel. These strafing runs were made even worst when the ammunition dump that the Taliban had seized exploded at the same time. Some said that the most powerful of those explosions opened all the doors on a twenty kilometres radius around the fortress!

With the help of 100 mm tank rounds...

Tuesday, November 27, 2001. The Taliban began to lose hope. According to the American Special Forces, only about fifty survivors who had no more water or ammunitions remained on the original six hundred their only food being limited to the hay of Dostom's cavalry horses. Some still try to escape, but they are very quickly arrested by the inhabitants who hang them from trees. The Alliance troops and the Special Forces then got ready to assault the south yard of the fortress. Seventeen of the nineteen American and British Special Forces took position on the roof of the main entrance, while the soldiers of the Northern Alliance were massed along the north side of the internal wall and on two sides of the entrance of the south yard. Furthermore, reinforcement troops were positioned behind the outside wall, south of the south yard. The plan aimed at attacking the Taliban from the north yard and from the south outside wall. The attack progressed in several stages, the attackers having to sometimes fall back when the defender's resistance proved too strong. Nevertheless, at about 12 o'clock, the Alliance troops took control of the portion of the yard that had been held by the Taliban as well as some parts of the internal buildings.

The Alliance forces were now sure of their victory, because the dif-

Top left. This buildings are located in the North yard of the Qala-e-Jangi prison; the picture was taken after the battle and taht part of the prison seeems to have been somewhat preserved from extensive damages. *(DOD Picture)*

Above. From the top of the eastern wall, a mixed group of US "Gree Berets", Delta Force operators and British SBS in "civvies" observe the f of 100 mm rounds fired over open sights by Northern Alliance's T55 tank on Talibans prisoners *(Getty/SIPA Press Picture*

Opposite page, from left to right: different pictures taken during the actu combats, showing the mercyless nature of that battle. It was a hand-t hand, no prisoner taken and no mercy expected furious affair involvir mortars, tanks and finally tactical air support. *(Jumbish+Milli Picture*

among this dishevelled bunch hid a twenty-year-old American Isla
convert!

The battle ended as it had started: by surrender. The surviving Ta
ban were taken away by three lorries.

This battle, considered as a massacre by some – which is complet
ly untrue, since the Taliban were armed and defended themselves fie
cely–was nevertheless the by-product of a series of error which deg
nerated into a full scale battle of an incredible intensity. In the first plac
the Taliban were never properly searched from the moment they ent
red the fortress. Secondly, when the revolt began, the number of guar
was woefully insufficient, on a ratio of probably one guard to four p
soners; furthermore, the Taliban were detained within twenty metr
of a huge Alliance arms and ammunitions dump. Thirdly, how can it b
explained that the two CIA agents never thought about arranging
proper "quick reaction force" to provide them with a modicum of pr
tection while carrying out the risky task of interrogating fanaticised isl
mist gunmen? This is an especially crucial question when one remem
bers that the two agents lost the radio equipment that was their onl
lifeline to the outside world very early in the fight, having then to rel
on the commandeered satellite telephone of a German TV crew tha
as luck would have it, was in the vicinity when the riot started.

The battle was won by the American and the British Special Fo

ferent rooms and yards of the fortress were literally covered with hundreds of dead or dying Taliban and foreign volunteers. Around two o'clock, the Alliance soldiers began to lose interest in the fight and started looting the corpses of the fallen islamist fighters. However, being still a bit too frightened to penetrate into the still Taliban-occupied stables, they preferred to send a T 55 tank forward which lobbed an extra five 100 mm shells into the ruins of those stables for good measure. The only surviving Taliban was finished off with stones... In the yard, Spann's body was found but the Taliban had had the time to booby-trap it with a hand grenade. At the end of the afternoon, the tactical part of the battle of Qala-e-Jangi was over. On Wednesday morning, general Dostom arrives from Kunduz to contemplate the slaughter.

The Special Forces' reaction

On Thursday November 29 2001, while collecting corpses, a member of an NGO was killed and several others were wounded, by several Taliban who were still hunkered down in the basements of the fortress. As an immediate response, the Alliance fighters fired several rockets into the tunnels to flush and eliminate them. Two days later,

Above. After the capture of Mazar-I-Sharif and the battle of Qala-e-Jangi, the US Special Forces had a much better idea of the exact fighting qualities of their Northern Alliance allies and they recruited more of them for the forthcoming battles. *(DOD Picture)*

Right. The American and British Special Forces decided to remain on situ on the wall of the fortress from Monday the 26th of November 2001. The western operators were occupying three different positions: one near the main entrance, another one under the North-Eastern watch tower and the last three hundred metres outside the North wall of the fortress. The real winners of that battle were the British and American Special Forces which, with the instrumental assistance of the tactical air support of American attack aircrafts, first stopped the Taliban uprising dead in its track and then cornered the islamists into a sector of the fortress were they almost all died fighting. *(ECPAD Picture)*

on Saturday, the Alliance soldiers finally decide to flood the underground passages to take out the last surviving Taliban, who were then thought to number no more than five or six.

But nothing could be further away from the truth. Around 11 AM, eighty-six starving survivors walked out from the dank cellars of the old fortress. To the American's utter surprise, they discovered that es who, operating alongside the Northern Alliance, really saved the day. It is true that the odds were stacked high against the Taliban who, once they realized they stood no chance of breaking free of the fortress, had no choice but to fight to the death, be crushed under the American airpower or surrender. The Taliban were stopped by the very prompt action of the Special Forces, which, in just a few hours, cornered them in a limited sector of the fortress where they could easily be submitted to the immense might of the US firepower.

For his action in the fortress, a British SBS sergeant has since been awarded the American Congressional Medal of Honor. Having volunteered to return with a small SBS team inside the fortress to try and extract "Dave", he was not able to perform his mission immediately but he still managed to stay inside the compound for several days, guiding air strikes that proved instrumental in the breaking of the Taliban's will to fight. It is also known that some of the Green Berets of the 5th SFG present during this battle received Purple Hearts for wounds received during that particular operation. Officially, those medals were awarded for having coordinated the air support during the battle of Qala-e-Jangi. The operators thus honoured have been presented to the press as Captains " Kevin " and "Paul", First Sergeant "David" and Sergeant First Class "Paul". One will note that, for reasons of operational security, their full names were not revealed.

Above. Tuesday the 27th of November 2001; the Talibans are now starting to lose hope. At this moment, the American Special Forces' estimate is that on the original six hundred prisoners, only about fifty survivors remain and that they are low on water and ammunition. *(Jumbish-i-Milli Picture)*

Right.
This battle is sometimes presented as a needless slaughter which is completely falacious. The Talibans were armed and they fought for their lives. What is on the other hand true is that it should never have taken place. Basic prisoner handling rules were violated and the end result was an extremly fierce battle that took days to conclude. *(Jumbish-i-Milli Picture)*

A CRUCIAL ROLE

Top, from left to right.
Series of shots showing MH-47E on operation. Without the shadow of a doubt,
160th SOAR was the Coalition special unit that, from mid-October 2001,
took part in all operations, day or night. For the "Night Stalkers"
of the 2nd battalion and for elements of the 1st battalion that had very discreetly
been deployed in Pakistan from October, the night time, low-altitude insertions
and extractions of special teams started on the19th of October.
(USSOCOM Pictures)

Left.
Two MH-47E helicopters belonging to the 160th Special Operations Aviation Regiment
on the Bagram air base, in the spring of 2002. The MH-47E is the most recent version
of the Chinook that is only in use with the Special Forces, the other Army Aviation units
flying the CH-47D version. 2/160, nicknamed Darkhorse, is the only unit in the world
to operate these helicopters. The MH-47E is fitted with three machine gun positions
that are fitted with two 7,62 mm Miniguns for the left and right door gunners
and a M 60D 7,62mm machine gun on the rear cargo ramp.
(Yves Debay Picture)

Bottom, from left to right.
Series of shots showing the "Night Stalkers" in action. Altogether,
during the first six months of the war, the 160th SOAR combat crews flew
more than 200 combat missions amounting to more than 2,000 combat flying hours.
Over seventy of those missions were insertions and extractions of special forces
teams deep inside Taliban country that were executed during the first three months
of the operations. That accumulated combat experience, mixed with the wealth of knowledge
of the crews all contribute to make the 160 SOAR the best special helicopter unit in the world.
(USSOCOM Pictures)

THE "NIGHT CENTAURS"

THE 160th Special Operations Aviation Regiment (Airborne)

The 160th Special Operations Aviation Regiment (Airborne) provides the U.S. Army with a unique air unit for night operations.

In the beginning, the 160th was formed from the 101st Aviation Battalion, 158th Aviation Batallion, 159th Aviation Batallion and 229th Aviation Batallion. For months these units trained in night flying and operational techniques, thus becoming the first "night" capacity air formation in the U.S. Army, under the name Task Force 160. The unit received official recognition on October 16, 1981 and was dubbed the 160th Aviation Battalion. Since that date the 160th is better known as the "Night Stalkers" because of its capacity for undertaking night operations and escaping detection.

Over the years the unit structure has been modified and in October 1986 the honorary title "Airborne" was added to its name. Then in June 1990, it became the 160th Special Operations Aviation Regiment (Airborne), including three battalions, an autonomous detachment and a National Guard battalion.

The 160th first came under fire in Grenada during Operation Urgent Fury, where it was able to accomplish its mission in spite of heavy fire from the Grenada and Cuban armed forces. In June, 1988, the helicopters from this unit participated in Operation Mount Hope III, then in Prime Chance, where the teams proved they could fly less than ten meters above the waves, at night, using night-vision binoculars and infrared markers.

The Night Stalkers were next called on to participate in Operation Just Cause in Panama, where they had to go directly from the winter climate of Fort Campbell to the equatorial weather of Panama. In 1993 the unit participated in Operation Restore Hope in Somalia and, with the Rangers and Delta Force soldiers, was able to accomplish several missions, including the famous operation portrayed in the film "The Fall of the Black Falcon", lasting more than 18 hours, and considered by the American Armed Forces to be the hardest fighting since the Vietnam War.

Above and right.
160th SOAR, which always flies
the most sophisticated of the rotary
wings in service in the US Army
Aviation has the reputation of being
the most efficient and experimented
Aviation unit of the US Armed forces.
On those views, two MH-60Ks
of the 160th SOAR are seen on the
Bagram airbase after
the "Night Stalkers" moved in from
Pakistan and Uzbekistan.
(Yves Debay Picture)

Without a doubt, during the Afghan conflict, the 160th Special Operations Aviation Regiment was the SF unit that was the most regularly involved in special operations, taking part in almost all of the Coalition's operations from the beginning of its deployment in mid-October 2001.

Indeed, the Night Stalkers of the 2nd battalion (or 2/160) and elements of the 1st battalion (1/160), were discreetly deployed in Pakistan, starting to fly their low altitude nocturnal special missions over Afghanistan from the evening of October the 19th in order to insert SF teams in the Taliban's back yard.

Once the Taliban had been ousted from power in Afghanistan, the 160th SOAR two units set up their quarters in Bagram and in Kandahar, their two main bases, and on several other advanced bases in the southeast of Afghanistan. During the campaign, USSOCOM commanders elected to use mostly the MH-47E and MH-60K helicopters, rather than the tiny and much handier MH-6 and AH-6J that really suffered from a lack of range, payload and power in the specific flying conditions in Afghanistan (altitude, heat, dust).

The best helicopter unit in the world

The twenty six MH-47E of 2/160 gave sterling service to the special forces of the Coalition, particularly since the MH-47E can fly with a full load up to 4 000 metres and can fly for over four hours without refuelling. "*I never was afraid during our missions in Afghanistan*", said an MH-47E pilot on his return to Fort Campbell, "*because we did receive fairly extensive damage to our choppers but they continued to fly without any problem. My only fear was the RPGs that were shot at us when we flew along the bottom of valleys that were under "Al-Qaida" positions located higher in the mountains.*"

160th SOAR has probably been of the most overworked units of

160th SOAR crewmember.
This reconstruction of an 160th SOAR MH-47E crewchief is dressed in a standard woodland camouflage BDU over which an OTV body armour fitted with additional armour plates and MOLLE ammo pouches for his MP-5 PDW submachine gun are worn. A "bungee cord" is attached to his harness in order to act as a lifeline between the crewmember and the helicopter during violent evasive actions while under fire. The black SPH-4 helmet fitted with a COBB mount for the AN/AVS-6/9 night vision goggles is fairly typical of 160th SOAR operators even though is it currently being replaced by a more modern type.

the American Army in the past eighteen months, being heavily engaged on several different theatres at the same time, deploying helicopters in Afghanistan and the Philippines were one of its MH-47E was lost to an accident. Another MH-47E was forced to the ground and destroyed in Afghanistan and three others were severely damaged. Five other MH-47E are currently based in the Republic of Korea.

The Night Stalkers were of course engaged in the Tora Bora operations, they participated in Operations Anaconda (with the Takur Ghar and Razor 01 tragedy, see boxed page 62, Condor, Buzzard, Mountain Lion and Mountain Sweep, to mention but the most important)

On the whole, during the first six months of the war, the Night Stalkers flew more than two hundred combat missions, clocking more than two thousand hours of combat flying. Of those 200 missions, over seventy were flown during the first three months to insert and extract Coalition's Special Forces behind Taliban lines. These months of operations have added to the intensive training of this unit to turn it into what probably is today the best special force helicopter unit in the world.

160th SOAR crewmember.
This reconstruction of an 160th SOAR MH-47E crewchief is dressed in the CWU-27/P tan colour flight suit and Nomex aviator gloves. Under his SARVIP vest (a MOLLE derivative) on which he has affixed a medic pouch, an M84 holster for his M9 pistol and a bayonet, he wears a class 4 body armour fitted with additional plates. The helmet is an SPH-4 fitted with a double visor, provisions for the fitting of a set of AN/AVS-6/9 night vision goggles and a Strobe light. That type of helmet has now been almost entirely replaced by the newer HGU-56 but some crewmembers preferred the SPH-4 over the newer type. A "bungee cord" is also visible attached to his harness; it acts as a lifeline between the crewmember and the helicopter during violent evasive actions while under fire.
The M-4 rifle is used to provide all-round security when landing in hostile areas or in case of a crash behind enemy lines.

Above. Two 160th SOAR MH-47Es sitting on the Bagram airstrip. The 2nd of March 2002 was a black day for American special forces in general and for this unit in particular. The missions of call signs *Razor 0.* and *Razor 02* that initially consisted in the insertion of special forces teams a the southernmost tip of the Shah-e-Kot valley turned into a series of ugly hand-to-hand firefights that resulted in the complete write-off of two MH-47Es and the loss of several American soldiers. *(Yves Debay Picture)*

From left to right. 160th SOAR has within its ranks the most sever hand-picked crews of the US Army Aviation. They are all capable of flyir at night at very very low altitude and in all weather condition *(USSOCOM Pictur*

A US Army Special Forces team boarding a 160th SOAR MH-60K. 160 SOAR mostly operated from Bagram and Kandahar but also used a seri of forward operation bases in the South-East of Afghanistan. USSOCO decided to mostly deploy MH-47Es and MH-60Ks in Afghanistan rather tha the tiny MH-6 and AH-6 that are both extremly agile but lacked range ar power in the "hot and high" conditions of Afghanistan. *(DOD Pictur*

Less than a week after 9/11, just like the rest of the US SF community, all the components of the Navy special units were on maximum alert. The USA were now at war. From mid-October, SEAL Team three which area of operation includes Central Asia was ready to operate in and around Afghanistan. SEAL Teams Three and Eight were ready to reinforce or replace ST3 after its first deployment that was to finish in January 2003. Each SEAL Team has, in peace time, a designated Area of Operations but they can be altered by USSOCOM if war requirements makes it a necessity.

Fifteen days before the first Special Forces teams were inserted into Afghanistan, the ST3 operators were already on board USS Kitty Hawk, an aircraft carrier that had been crammed full of special operation helicopters and operators. This carrier was to serve as a rear base for special operations in the South and in the West of Afghanistan because at that time, negotiations were still underway between the Americans and the Pakistani on the use of Pakistani air bases as forward operating bases for US special forces. The Americans exerted a pressure on the Pakistani to reach an agreement because they wanted to be able to bring their troops as close to Afghanistan as possible and in relatively safe and discreet surroundings.

Left.
A SSE (Sensitive Site Exploration) mission undertaken by Navy SEALs in the Jaji mountains on the 12th of February 2002. In SF parlance, an SSE is an operation undertaken by special operators acting on specific tips in a "hot" area. In six months of operations, twenty "contacts" and nearly forty reconnaissance missions, SEAL platoons suffered no casualties.
(USN Picture)

Bottom, from left to right.
Series of pictures presenting the results of a Taliban commander cave search by US special operators including Navy SEALs a hundred kilometres north Kandahar on the 12th of May 2002. During this operation, five Taliban were killed and thirty-two captured. Recoilless rifles and anti aircraft missiles can be noticed among the seized weapons as well as many documents.
(CENTCOM Picture)

Navy SEAL during a search mission in the South East of Afghanistan in February 2002.
The US Navy was well represented by its SEAL operators in the Afghan theatre of operation. This SEAL team member is wearing a non-regulation "uniform" composed of an issue desert BDU trousers, a black fleece jacket, a rappelling harness and a woodland camouflage boonie hat. The load bearing equipment is a modified TLBV altered by the addition of horizontal pockets, of a double pistol magazine pouch on the left shoulder and of an SDU-5/E Strobe Light on the right shoulder. His SEAL-specific gloves are made of a combination of Nomex and neoprene. This operator is armed with a Benelli M3 semi-automatic 12 gauge shotgun which is particularly useful for tunnel clearing and a HK Mark 23 SOCOM .45 ACP pistol.

Failure in Tora Bora

Once Islamabad had agreed to the American deployment on its soil, all the SEAL Teams were to move to Pakistan. But the rapid collapse of the Taliban regime at the beginning of November rendered all the initial planning useless; the majority of operations which had already been planned for SEAL teams had to be cancelled. By mid-December, the CENTCOM planners in Tampa Florida decide it is time for the SEALs to be deployed operationally; by this time, the Special Forces, the Delta Force and the Rangers have already been on the ground since mid-October and the strain of continuous operations was starting to show. Several SEAL operators organized in small reconnaissance

Above.
Task Force K-Bar US Navy SEALs checking crates of ammunition uncovered in "Al Qaida" caches in the Jaji mountains. During that period, the SEALs undertook at least a dozen site reconnaissance and house searches operations alongside German KSK commandos. One of those KSK commandos is barely visible in the right hand corner of the picture in his distinctive "Flecktarn" desert camouflage.
(DOD Picture)

Right, from top to bottom.
Some of the weapons uncovered in January 2002 by SEAL operators from SEAL Team 3 in the South East of Afghanistan.
(USN Picture)

SEAL team members and EOD specialists about to blow up a Taliban ammunition dump. US special operators found hundred of such dumps in the South and South East of Afghanistan.

Example of such an ammunition dump built with Western support by Mudjahidins during the "Soviet War".
(DOD Picture)

Next page, top left.
In the vicinity of Kandahar, in one of the numerous weapon dumps built by the Taliban, a SEAL presents crates of artillery and aviation ammunition the Taliban left intact in their hasty retreat. During their first ten months in Afghanistan, platoons from SEAL Teams 2, 3, 8 and SDW-1 (Swimmer Delivery Vehicle) operated in and around Afghanistan.
(USN Picture)

Next page, top right.
A US Navy ordnance specialist attached to a Navy special warfare detachment shows some of the ammunition uncovered during a search before blowing them up.
(USN Picture)

SEAL during Operation *Anaconda*.
The SEALs were heavily involved in *Operation Anaconda*.
They lost a team member in Takur Ghar when he fell from an MH-47E; this operator fought alone until killed by "Al Qaida" gunmen. Like other special operators, the SEALs dressed in modified BDUs which are completed, in this reconstruction, by civilian mountain boots and knee pads which were popular for operations in rocky areas. Even though hot, body armour were worn, completed here by a RACK system to carry "link" ammunition for the M-60E3. The M-60 has now been replaced by the M-240B in the American armed forces but the SEALs still use the M-60E3 because they appreciate its compactness and its resistance to saline environment. The secondary weapon is an HK Mark 23 pistol. In the occurrence CS gas are used to clear a tunnel, an M40 gas mask is carried in an Eagle thigh pouch.

The Naval Special Warfare Command

Headquartered in Coronado California, the Naval Special Warfare Command is 4950 active duty and 1200 reserve personnel strong. The US Navy special units are broken down into SEAL (Sea Air Land) Teams, Special Boat Units (SBU) and SEAL Delivery Vehicle units. They are spread between the East and the West coasts.

Among the active duty personnel, 2500 are SEALs, 500 are SBUs, 200 are SDVs and another 1750 are Navy technicians.

A SEAL Team is a US Navy special force unit. A SEAL platoon is made up of sixteen operators and it can perform all sorts of naval reconnaissance, beach clearing or covert missions depending on the task at hand. A SEAL platoon and an SBU detachment are included in all US Marine Corps deployments of Marine Amphibious Ready Group as well as within the Task Forces including an aircraft carrier deployed from the East Coast. A SEAL platoon is also dedicated to the West Coast but it is only deployed in some specific circumstances.

For the Afghan campaign, the country being landlocked, the SEALs used helicopters as their main workhorse.

Top right picture.
A SEAL Team 3 member observing
the blowing up of a dump of "Al Qaida"
ammunition uncovered in the mountains
of the South East of Afghanistan
just before the beginning of Operation
Anaconda. During this operation,
SEAL Teams undertook a number
of reconnaissance missions, including
the ill-fated Takur Ghar mission
on March the 4th 2002.
(DOD Picture)

Some figures on the SEAL Teams

By the end of July 2002, SEAL Teams had already undertaken 23 combat operations, 45 reconnaissance missions, 12 underwater suspect ships hull inspections, 150 requests for tactical air support; they also had captured 110 gunmen and killed 115 others for the loss of 2 operators, two others having also been wounded.

SEAL Team member during a search operation in the Jaji mountain villages.
This operator is muffled against the cold in a SPEAR/USSOCOM fleece, a Nomex hood and Oakley Assault goggles. His rations, spare ammunitions and specialized equipment are carried in a woodland camouflage Eagle A III Pack and he is armed with the ubiquitous M-4 fitted with an Aimpoint red-dot sight and a SureFire torch as well as the regulation M9 Beretta pistol in a Safariland SLS holster.

SEAL Team member during a CQB (Close Quarter Battle) operation
The SEAL teams tend to use a specific "rig" for that type of operation; it is composed of a Nomex flight suit and a Class 3 body armour over which is worn an assault vest the type of which being left to the operator's appreciation. In this reconstruction the operator wears a RACK vest for its light weight and the freedom of action it affords his equipment is completed by a rappelling harness, Bollé tactical goggles, a Protec helmet and Blackhawk knee pads. His weapons is an M-4 fitted with a RIS and a VLI torch the M-4 is preferred over the MP-5 for the power of its 5,56 mm rounds. Each SEAL Team member is also equipped with a PRC-127 radio with PTT/VOX microphone and earpiece

teams were then inserted in the Tora Bora mountains to report on Taliban operations and movements and to guide tactical air support aircraft. As it has already been extensively reported, this operation, which had been decided in accordance with the Afghan allies, was a failure; Ussama Ben Laden and his main subordinate commanders managed to escape the loose net that had been cast around their positions. After British SAS and US Navy SEAL reports of the failing of that system, CENTCOM decided that from then on, operations would only be trusted to Coalition forces.

Caves and tunnels

That type of operation started barely a month later in January 2002 in the South East of Afghanistan. The SEAL Teams operated alongside foreign special operators including German KSK commandos during ten days, searching caves and tunnels in the Zhawar Kili area. During those operations, the SEALs seized a number of relatively sophisticated weapons as well as masses of documents

some pertaining to the internal functioning of "Al Qaida".

In Zhawar Kili, a SEAL platoon composed of two officers and fourteen petty officers and mates reinforced by two USAF Combat Controllers was sent into this area for a mission that was originally planned to last for twelve hours.

Nine days later, having had to feed on livestock abandoned by "Al-Qaida" in its retreat and drinking water they had to purify with their survival kit, the SEALs came back to their base after having been re-tasked several times, searching over seventy caves and tunnels in a six kilometres by six kilometres area! If most of those caves were in fact deserted, eight terrorists were none the less captured and weapons and documents were once again seized in large quantities. Once the searches were completed, tactical air support was called to

Above.
The casket of US Navy Petty Officer 1st Class Neil C. Roberts, age 32, from SEAL Team 2 being offloaded from a USAF C-130. He had been killed in action in the Takur Ghar mountains on March the 4th 2002 after falling from an MH-47E. After having expanded all his ammunition, he was killed by some "Al Qaida" gunmen. *(DOD Picture)*

Right.
Two SEAL Team members doing the reconnaissance of a suspect site near the border with Pakistan. In the Spring of 2002, US Navy SEALs undertook a splendid heliborne operation when, with the support of Danish commandos, and within an hour of receiving the intelligence tip, they managed to locate and intercept a vehicular convoy in which they captured one of Ben Laden's Lieutenant, Mullah Khairullah. *(USN Picture)*

Composition of the Joint Special Operations Task Force Ever in Afghanistan

Between November 2001 and July 2002, the Joint Special Operations Task Force Ever (JSOTF Ever), under the command of Captain Calland from the Naval Special Warfare was made up of the following units (this list includes some European special units that were attached to it at a latter date):

- platoons from SEAL Teams 2, 3, 8 and SDV-1
- elements from the 4th Psychological Operations Group
- USAF CCTs and Pararescuemen
- 160th SOAR and USMC CH-53 helicopters
- 100 Danish special forces
- 100 German KSK Commandos
- 40 NZ SAS
- 40 Canadian special forces from JTF-2
- 50 Norwegian Jaeger Kommandos
- 28 Norwegian Marine Jaeger Kommandos
- 95 Australian SAS

Opposite left, top to bottom. In position outside a suspect village, a SEAL is aiming his M4 to cover the progression of his combat group during winter of 2001-2002. At that time, the Navy Task Force included SEAL and German, Norwegian and Danish Special Forces. Shock troops that according to the CENTCOM, « got results ». This fighter has a Black Hawk Camelback. *(USN Picture)*

Mountainside meeting between a SEAL team and a village chief during the winter 2001-2002 operations. Progression is difficult, not only because of the terrain and the climate, and supply problems for the deployed units, but also because of opposition coming from Taliban fighters and «Al-Qaida » members still hiding out in the areas near the Pakistan border.

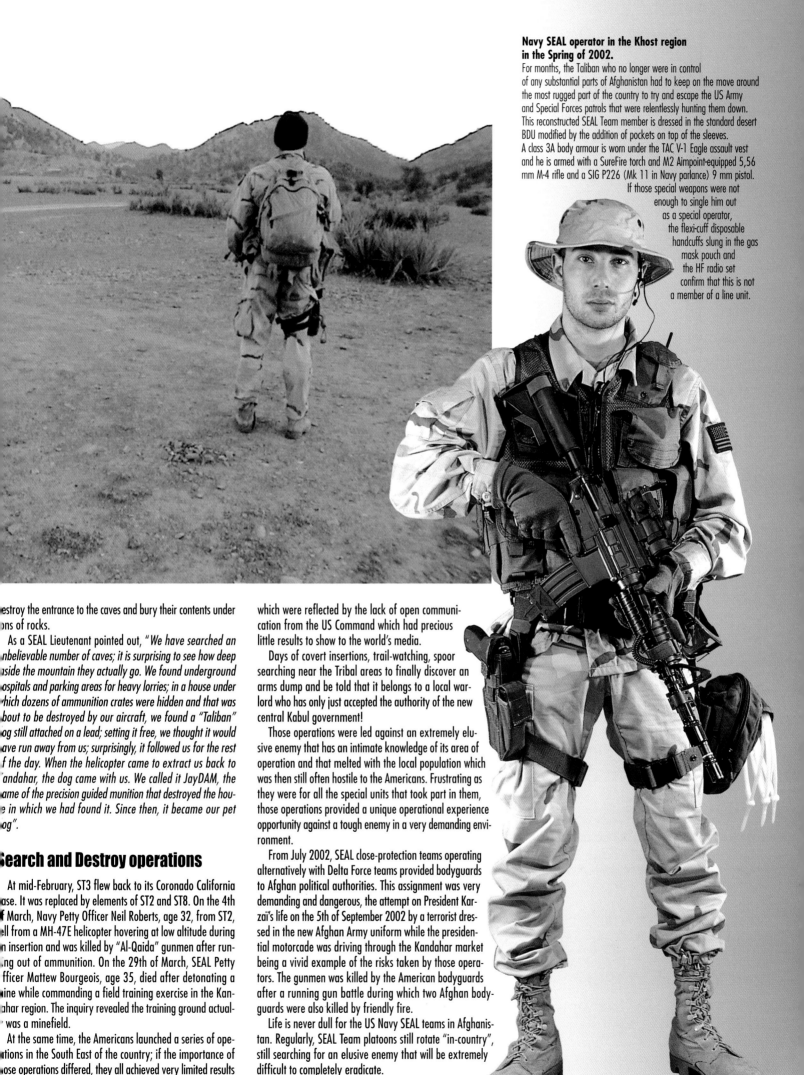

Navy SEAL operator in the Khost region in the Spring of 2002.
For months, the Taliban who no longer were in control of any substantial parts of Afghanistan had to keep on the move around the most rugged part of the country to try and escape the US Army and Special Forces patrols that were relentlessly hunting them down. This reconstructed SEAL Team member is dressed in the standard desert BDU modified by the addition of pockets on top of the sleeves. A class 3A body armour is worn under the TAC V-1 Eagle assault vest and he is armed with a SureFire torch and M2 Aimpoint-equipped 5,56 mm M-4 rifle and a SIG P226 (Mk 11 in Navy parlance) 9 mm pistol. If those special weapons were not enough to single him out as a special operator, the flexi-cuff disposable handcuffs slung in the gas mask pouch and the HF radio set confirm that this is not a member of a line unit.

estroy the entrance to the caves and bury their contents under
ons of rocks.

As a SEAL Lieutenant pointed out, "*We have searched an
nbelievable number of caves; it is surprising to see how deep
nside the mountain they actually go. We found underground
ospitals and parking areas for heavy lorries; in a house under
hich dozens of ammunition crates were hidden and that was
bout to be destroyed by our aircraft, we found a "Taliban"
og still attached on a lead; setting it free, we thought it would
ave run away from us; surprisingly, it followed us for the rest
f the day. When the helicopter came to extract us back to
andahar, the dog came with us. We called it JayDAM, the
ame of the precision guided munition that destroyed the hou-
e in which we had found it. Since then, it became our pet
og".*

earch and Destroy operations

At mid-February, ST3 flew back to its Coronado California
ase. It was replaced by elements of ST2 and ST8. On the 4th
f March, Navy Petty Officer Neil Roberts, age 32, from ST2,
ll from a MH-47E helicopter hovering at low altitude during
n insertion and was killed by "Al-Qaida" gunmen after run-
ng out of ammunition. On the 29th of March, SEAL Petty
fficer Mattew Bourgeois, age 35, died after detonating a
ine while commanding a field training exercise in the Kan-
ahar region. The inquiry revealed the training ground actual-
was a minefield.

At the same time, the Americans launched a series of ope-
tions in the South East of the country; if the importance of
ose operations differed, they all achieved very limited results

which were reflected by the lack of open communication from the US Command which had precious
little results to show to the world's media.

Days of covert insertions, trail-watching, spoor
searching near the Tribal areas to finally discover an
arms dump and be told that it belongs to a local warlord who has only just accepted the authority of the new
central Kabul government!

Those operations were led against an extremely elusive enemy that has an intimate knowledge of its area of
operation and that melted with the local population which
was then still often hostile to the Americans. Frustrating as
they were for all the special units that took part in them,
those operations provided a unique operational experience
opportunity against a tough enemy in a very demanding environment.

From July 2002, SEAL close-protection teams operating
alternatively with Delta Force teams provided bodyguards
to Afghan political authorities. This assignment was very
demanding and dangerous, the attempt on President Karzaï's life on the 5th of September 2002 by a terrorist dressed in the new Afghan Army uniform while the presidential motorcade was driving through the Kandahar market
being a vivid example of the risks taken by those operators. The gunmen was killed by the American bodyguards
after a running gun battle during which two Afghan bodyguards were also killed by friendly fire.

Life is never dull for the US Navy SEAL teams in Afghanistan. Regularly, SEAL Team platoons still rotate "in-country",
still searching for an elusive enemy that will be extremely
difficult to completely eradicate.

EART OF MARITIME COUNTER-TERRORISM

The White House insisted that the aircraft-carrier USS Kitty Hawk be used as headquarters and departure base for special operations in Afghanistan.

Psychologically, as President Bush said, this war was different, so things had to be done differently. Usually special operations were undertaken from ground-based platforms.

The Kitty Hawk was operational in the Indian Ocean from October 13, 2001 on. So special operations were directed from this aircraft-carrier. In the war area, at least, since orders still came from the Central Command in Tampa, Florida. In this same zone all of the different Task Force ships could be found, with their SEAL teams and Special Boat Units that had been borrowed from their respective groups for maritime counter-terrorism missions.

Disappointing results

The most important mission was naturally searching the innumerable ships cruising in the zone, in liaison with other special naval units, Australian, Spanish, German, British and French.

Thus from October 2001 to the end of 2002, the Navy Task Force ships cruised the waters of the Indian Ocean and the Persian Gulf looking for terrorists. The results were globally disappointing, and Washington decided, from the fall of 2002 on, to reposition her naval units in preparation for an attack against Iraq. SEAL teams and boarding crews specially trained for searching ships continued to operate in the Persian Gulf tracking ships going into or out of Iraq in violation of Security Council Resolution 986.

Opposite. Dropping a SEAL team from Little Creek, Virginia, on the deck of an assault vessel, the USS Oscar Austin (DDG 79), using SH-60B Seahawk helicopters. This type of action is possible on a ship with a relatively large deck, such as a tanker or a cruise-ship, and requires perfect coordination between the helicopters and the aircraft providing cover for the action.
(*US Navy Picture*)

Lower left. Checking a ship suspected of ties with "Al-Qaida". The RHIB- (Rigid-Hulled Inflatable Boat) type craft from Navy Special Warfare is travelling slowly. She is heavily armed for a boat of this size, with two 12.7-mm machine guns.
(*US Navy Picture*)

Navy SEAL equiped for a maritime counter-terrorism night operation.
The black BDU clothing is preferable to a warmer jump suit. The exclusively "silent" weapons include the famous 9-mm HK MP-5-SD6 automatic pistol and the 45-cal. SOCOM Mk23 pistol equiped with a LAM (Laser Aiming Module) emitting visible or infrared laser light, carried in a Wilcox type II hip pack. The K-Bar II knife stuck into his belt can be used if necessary in CQB combat or to knife a sentry. A class-3 flak vest offers protection against most of the calibers typically found in combat situations. The TAC-VI-NU Eagle jacket allows him to carry his supplies : ammunition, radio, first aid kit. A Nomex hood and gloves complete the equipment. In order to gain a tactical advantage, our SEAL is using the third-generation PVS-18 monocle, capable of under-water vision up to a depth of 20 meters. This type of instrument combines natural vision and night vision for a larger viewing angle. The face harness can also be used with the A and C versions of the PVS-7, used exclusively by the SEALs.

Above and opposite. Somewhere in the Indian Ocean, SEALs rope down from a MH-Pave Low onto the deck of the USS Mount Whitney (LCC/JCC 20), and follow-up with rapid single-file progression. This type of operation was undertaken several times aboard suspect merchant ships, but without significant results, at least as far as tracking "Al-Qaida" members is concerned. These operations were repeated in the Persian Gulf against Iraq as part of missions resulting from the United Nations Security Council resolutions. *(US Navy Picture)*

Following page. Helicopter cluster exercise, known as Special Purpose Insertion/Extraction (SPIE), above the flight deck of the USS John Kennedy (CV 67) before it moves out to relieve the USS Theodore Roosevelt (CV 71), as part of Operation Enduring Freedom. The SEAL teams regularly perform this type of exercise, allowing the commandos to be dropped rapidly and furtively onto an undefended enemy platform. *(Photo US Navy)*

NAVSPECWARGRU

NAVSPECWARGRU 1 is made up of
● SEAL Teams 1 , 3 and 5,
● Special Boat Squadron 1
● SVD TEAM 1.

NAVSPECWARGRU 2, the headquarters of which being situated in Little Creek, Virginia and who has an area of responsibility ranging from the Atlantic Ocean to Latin America and Europe, is made up
● SEAL Teams 2 , 4 and 8,
● Special Boat Squadron 2
● SVD TEAM 2.

DELTA FORCE IN ACTION

At the beginning of October 2001, about ten Delta Force A, and C Squadron teams were already on the ground around Afghanistan. They were based in Uzbekistan, in Tajikistan and in Pakistan, in safe houses located near the various air bases lent to the United States by these countries.

The main mission of these "super commandos" was to seize the "Al-Qaida" leader and his main lieutenants, as well as mullah Omar, the talibans leader, and his commanders. The other missions were labelled as such: free the Western hostages held in Kabul and in Kandahar by the Taliban and support the American special forces teams which will were going to be inserted in Afghanistan in order to operate alongside the Northern Alliance troops.

Events heated up from October 15 when Washington decided to intensify the air bombardment and to infiltrate Special Forces teams in the North and the southwest of Afghanistan. At the same time, a joint "media and SOF" operation was planned to try and seize mullah Omar and his main accomplices who had been tracked down some kilometres from Kandahar.

"The bird has flown away"

During the night of October 19, 160th Special Operations Aviation Regiment helicopters took off from the Pakistani bases of Dobandin and Samungli loaded with Delta Force operators; nap-of-the-earth, they raced towards mullah Omar's den. South of them some MC130Hs which had taken off from Oman a few hours previously got ready to parachute about a hundred Rangers from the 75th Ranger Regiment around a hundred kilometres southwest

The Pentagon's covert action specialists pool

First SFOD-Delta (Special Force Operations Delta) or Delta Forces is one of the most secret American antiterrorist units. The Pentagon keeps all information pertaining to this unit under a thick veil of secrecy.

Also called CAG for Combat Application Group, it is composed of soldiers officially recruited from every branch of the Army but who mostly stem from either Ranger Battalions or Special Forces units. SFOD-D, or whichever name it is using at any given time, is located in a special compound in Fort Bragg, North Carolina.

Depending on sources, a total figure of about 2 000 is often quoted for the total strength of the unit; but one must keep in mind the fact that SFOD-D can and does tailor its units to the missions it receives and this makes for a flexible establishment. In a way, SFOD-D is more like a provider of very well trained operators, men and women, to which the command can resort to when it needs to. In theory, Delta Force consist of three operational groups: a support and communications group, a "mixed" group called the Funny Platoon because it is made up of both male and female operators which makes SFOD-D unique within the JSOC and, finally, an aviation group regrouping an unspecified number of aircrafts and helicopters.

Although Delta Forces often works with the 160th Special Operations Aviation Regiment (SOAR), it also possesses a number of rotary and fixed wings aircrafts in the colours of civilian airline companies created for the occasion. The helicopters are used for the transport of the operators as well as in the "Gunship" role when equipped with gun or/and rockets pods. This almost complete freedom of action also comes from the fact that Delta can sometimes be called to work with the CIA's Special Operations Group.

Delta's main mission, and it is hardly surprising since it was created originally as an antiterrorist group, is hostages' liberation. To hone their skills in that field to an ever-increasing sharpness, Delta possesses, in its Fort Bragg compound, special training areas that recreate all the possible tactical scenarios they could face. Houses, buses, aircrafts, all those possibilities and many more are studied in depths, alone or with other world renowned groups like the British SAS and SBS who have installations similar to these but probably nowhere as modern.

ted it an hour before. During the return flight at very low-level, an MH60 lost the wheels of its landing gear on an obstacle, whereas an MH-53J Pave Low loaded with Rangers crashed to the ground near Kandahar. Fortunately, no one was killed.

This operation did not go unnoticed by the Taliban who, of course, claimed to have routed the Americans. The truth is that Washington wanted a spectacular special force operation to happen fairly early in the campaign to show the Taliban they could strike at will. The problem was that the Delta operators were supposed to leave a "stay-behind" party at the end of the first part of the operation to monitor the Taliban's movement in the area. In reality, this "stay-behind" party had to be exfiltrated with the main body because the operators supposedly reported that the area was literally crawling with Taliban and was deemed to be too dangerous.

On this very same night, dozens of Special Forces teams were helicoptered into the North of Afghanistan. Among them were some Delta operators who had been especially tasked with the training and advising of the most capable military governors of the Northern Alliance. After

Kandahar in a deception operation meant to focus the enemy's attention away from Delta's operations. As soon as the Delta operators hit the ground, they started searching the buildings, eliminating sentries along the way. But their target was not there. A few kilometres from the scene, several Pave Low helicopters filled with Rangers were waiting, ready to intervene and lend a hand in cases things started getting sour. But, apart from a few scattered exchanges of fire (AKMs and RPGs), the resistance was almost nil; considering several AC-130s had obliterated the scene before the insertion, that was hardly surprising. After a search of the building that left, in the eyes of some experts, much to be desired, the Delta element was then extracted by the same helicopters that had inser-

Top right.
Delta Force close protection detail providing immediate security for a group of American field grade officers during a meeting with Afghan dignitaries in Spinboldak, a zone close to the Pakistani border often travelled by Taliban and "Al-Qaida" volunteers. It is possible to notice the considerable leeway afforded to those operators for whom only results count. Dress regulations and codes obviously don't apply to these unconventional soldiers.
(SIPA/Press Picture)

Below left.
On January 27, 2002 two operators probably belonging to Delta Forces are caught on camera clearing the buildings of the Kandahar hospital that was then still in the hands of a stubborn group of "Al-Qaida" gunmen.
(Freedomnews Picture)

Delta Force member during an anti-Taliban operation.
The Delta Force participated, along with its Navy and Army counterparts, in the hunt for the Talibans. The prime target is of course the head of "Al-Qaida" and his lieutenants. The soldiers' dress was definitely non-regimental, which allowed them to live up to their reputation as « tough guys » and super-fighters. Nothing indicates that this soldier is a Delta Force member. The Woodland camouflage jacket at least allows him to be identified as a US soldier, as do the Beretta M9 in his belt or the Stoner SR-15, an adaptation of the M4. His pants are civilian, designed for mountain-hiking, as are his boots. The Shemag offers a slight protection against the cold, but mainly allows the American soldiers "to blend in" with the fighters of the Northern Alliance.

that, events really accelerated, the Northern Alliance launching its military operations against Mazar-e-Sharif from November 4, 2001, and Kabul falling less than ten days later. Delta participated in several actions officially — that is operations media got wind of — as Special Forces; then it became even harder to track them down (nothing new there!); they have been rumoured to have taken part in the operations in and around the Qala-e-Jangi prison (November 25-27) and in the Tora Bora area (at the beginning of December).

A perfect operation

Sunday, January 27, 2002, Kandahar hospital. 17. 50. The silence of the dusty Kandahar hospital, in the South of Afghanistan, is suddenly shattered by bursts from automatic weapons followed by grenade explosions. Officially, Afghan soldiers with their American advisors — in reality Delta operators - try to arrest or kill six Arabic fighters of " Al-Qaida " who took refuge in one of the hospital's buildings.

An American accented voice roars: "Go! Go!" Every room is systematically cleared with grenades and bursts of automatic weapons. It is true that, prior to the operation being launched, the Islamist fighters had, for several hours refused to negotiate and surrender. In front of such behaviour, the Delta element leader decided to finish the "job". The Tampa command knows that the Arabic fighters are ready to sell their lives dearly: only one month before, one of them had tried to escape from the same hospital using his black turban as a rope; just before being arrested again, he had chosen to blow himself up with a grenade.

In mid-December 2001, SF and Delta operators have ju reached the Pakistani border in the Spinboldak are the Taliban regime is crumbling but armed detachmen are still aggressive near Kandah and in the South of Afghanista (SIPA Press Pictur

Delta Force, Kandahar, January, 2002.
During the fall of Kandahar, the Talibans sought refuge in the hospi buildings. The major part of the American troops fighting them wer Delta Force soldiers. The CQB (Close Quarter Battle) attire of the De is similar to that of the SEALs : CWU-27 fatigues, flak vest, tactical kneepads, harness belt, gas mask, knife . . .
The weapons always include an M4, with a Glock 17, a P226 or a as a hand gun. The Protec helmet can be varied : here it is the hal version, with an unofficial COBB mount designed to carry a JVN AN or an F5050, the ground version of the ANVIS.

In order to make this undertaking look like a joint American and Afghan operation, the Americans tried to persuade the media that the Afghans had led the assault. In reality, when the last ultimatum expired at 2 o'clock in the morning, the Delta operators first assaulted the building on their own. Using night-vision goggles, supported by several snipers posted on rooftops, they cleared the compound in fifteen minutes, killing all six terrorists. The witnesses declared to have seen a series of "flash-bang" grenades (concussion grenades designed to blind and disorientate any opponent located in the room where it has been thrown) going off, followed by successions of "double-taps" (two shots fired in quick succession on semi-automatic mode for better accuracy) for every target that appeared. All together, a splendidly prepared and executed operation that caused no civilian casualties in the hospital and, on the Coalition's side, only five Afghan soldiers being wounded during the operation.

Operations in and near Pakistan

On March 18, an operation conducted by Delta Forces was revealed to the press. About eighty kilometres away from Gardez and acting on intelligence gathered by one of the CIA Predator drones, a "heavy" team, so called because it packed a much heavier fire power than normal for a Delta team (Anti-tank missile launchers and automatic grenade launchers) was helicoptered, less than two hours after having been put on alert, on a pass leading into Pakistan. The mission consisted in intercepting a group of light vehicles 4 x 4 SUVs transporting " Al-Qaida " fighters and to arrest some of them. The results of that operation were self explanatory: all the vehicles were destroyed, four-

Delta Force sniper, Kandahar, January, 2002.
The snipers played a major role in the assault on the Kandahar hospital where the Talibans were hiding out. This Delta Force soldier is equiped with a SOCOM M24 rifle. The telescopic sight has lighted cross-hairs for shooting in the dark. A desert camouflage net has been placed around the weapon. An M9 PA will be used for close-up protection. The outfit is once again not exactly official ! : only the BDU pants allow this paratrooper to be identified as an American soldier.
Note the Leatherman tool hanging from the straps of the tactical hip pack.

teen Islamist gunmen were killed in less than a minute, only two fighters being arrested alive, of whom seriously wounded.

On May 26, 2002, ten Pakistani servicemen were killed during a raid led against a presumed "Al-Qaida" base in Waziristan (northwest of Pakistan); during the operation, several members of the terrorist organization were arrested and one killed. On the occasion of this raid, it seems that American special units, most probably Delta, operated in the region with their Pakistani intelligence counterparts to hunt down the Islamist terrorist.

It is fairly safe now to estimate that many of the operations in and near Pakistan against houses or zones sheltering "Al-Qaida's" members that have been attributed to the FBI or the CIA by the media have in fact been undertaken by Delta Force detachments.

Above, left to righ.
At the time of the assassination attempt against Afghan President Hamid Karzaï on Thursday, September 5, 2002. These Deltas are in charge of protecting the president, and maintaining a protective perimeter around the building housing the president after the attack .
(Ed Wray/ AP/SIPA-Press Picture)

Deltas carrying out close-up protection of an Afghan dignitary.
After the fall of Kabul and the Taliban regime, a new government was set up with Hamid Karzai as president. On September 5, 2002 a Taliban disguised as a soldier tried to kill him. The episode ended in a shoot-out, and the would-be killer, along with two of his body guards, were killed by Delta Force soldiers assigned to close-up protection of the president.
These men, in civilian clothing, are standing back behind the Afghan forces that made up the major part of the presidential protection team. The dazzling American Special Forces intervention was televised throughout the entire world.

Some Delta Force operations

Because of their very tight operational security rules, it is very difficult to know anything about SFOD-D's past operations. Only a few came to light, mostly for the embarrassment they have caused which is definitely not giving justice to this unit. The first "official" action of Delta took place during operation Just Cause in Panama, in December, 1989, when Delta Force teams were tasked with the rescuing of American businessman Kurt Muse in his prison in the city of Modelo.

During this operation, an assault team was inserted on the roof of the prison by an MH-6 helicopter of the 160th SOAR. In a few minutes, Delta managed to come down to the second floor, to blow the various cells doors up, one of which finally being that of Kurt Muse's, and to free him without any harm. While the antiterrorist team waited for the extraction helicopter, the ex-prisoner had time to realize that four of his former gaolers were dead and three others had been taken prisoners. The situation suddenly took a turn for the worst when the MH-6, loaded with its passengers, was hit by enemy fire and crashed down in a nearby street. Fortunately, the infrared lamp of one of the Delta operators alerted a UH-60 helicopter and it reported its position to a nearby American unit, provoking the quick dispatch of soldiers belonging to the US Army's 6th infantry regiment on to the crash scene. On the

whole, four Delta operators were wounded, the hostage was saved, and the existence of this very special unity was revealed to the public.

Then came a series of operations during Desert Storm in 1990-1991; Delta teams are rumoured to have undertaken several missions in Iraq in search of Scud Transporters-Erectors-Launchers (TELs); in Kurdistan, they were involved with anti-Saddam movements; in Saudi Arabia, they were tasked with the protection of general Norman Schwartzkopf.

Then, Delta Forces was committed to Restore Hope the disastrous and badly led UN operation in Somalia. After a string of successful operations that led to the arrest of several warlords in Mogadishu, the last arrest, on the 3rd of October, 1993, ended in a major gunfight that caused the death of three Delta operators, fifteen rangers, helicopter crews and Mountain soldiers and the destruction of two160th SOAR helicopters. This operation was immortalized by the "Black Hawk Down" film. In the following years, SFOD-D was nevertheless engaged in other operations in Macedonia, in Kosovo, in Afghanistan and in several bordering countries.

At the moment, it is very likely that Delta teams are active in Iraq, in the Philippines, in Saudi Arabia, and in Kenya.

THE BATTLE FOR TAKUR GHAR DURING

Very early on the morning of March 4, 2002 on a remote mountain top called Takur Ghar, in the southeast of Afghanistan, a group of "Al-Qaida" fighters opened fire on an MH-47E helicopter that was transporting an American Special Forces reconnaissance team. During the exchanges of fire, a US Navy SEAL fell from the helicopter and survived his fall. The scene was then set for the most intense combat operation the American Special Forces were to experience in Afghanistan. The immediate result of that encounter was the complete annihilation of this group of Islamist fighters, but also the death of seven American soldiers.

This battle was also marked by the human quality of the Army, Navy and the Air Force Special Forces personnel who never hesitated to take very high personal risks in order not to leave the body of one of their fallen comrades in the hands of the enemy.

Everything began a fortnight earlier when General Hagenbeck, who was then in command of Task Force Mountain decided to launch *operation Anaconda*. Very traditional in its approach, *Operation Anaconda* was conceived around the tried and tested concept of the hammer and the anvil and it aimed at the annihilation of several Taliban pockets of resistance that had been located in the Shah-e-Kot valley, southeast of the city of Gardez. The concept of operation was to flush the Taliban towards the positions held by soldiers of the 10th Mountain Division and of the 101st Airborne Division that were located in the eastern part of the valley. The US command had planned to place recce teams on key points and it had tasked those teams with the location of fleeing enemy and the guiding of coalition attack aircraft. That tactic did work in several areas and it achieved the destruction of "Al-Qaida" positions and the death of hundreds of enemy gunmen, particularly in the Shah-e-Kot sector.

However, as everybody in the armed forces knows, no plan survives contact with the enemy. Instead of running away, well armed and equipped "Al-Qaida" groups, often reinforced by local villagers, decided to dig in and fight were they stood. First of all, they managed to stop and drive back the Afghan governmental forces; then, poor weather prevented the Americans from flying in their units to the desired positions in time. Trying to reorganize his forces in the valley of Shah-e-Kot, General Hagenbeck decided that he needed more observation posts on the towering peaks above him. At three thousand metres above sea level, the Takur Ghar mountain appeared to an ideal location for a Special Forces team. Regrettably for the Americans, the "Al-Qaida" fighters had had the same idea, setting up on that mountaintop a heavy machine gun capable of firing at the Coalition planes that were flying down in the valley.

On March 2, 2002 the American staff decided that two observation posts would be set up the next night, the helicopter lift being provided by two MH-47E belonging to the 2nd Battalion of the 160th Operations Aviation Regiment (Airborne). The first MH47E, call sign Razor 04 was to drop a team north of the summit, whereas the second, Razor 03 was to directly insert a mixed team of US Navy SEALs and USAF CCT on top of Takur Ghar.

At about 3 o'clock (local time), Razor 03 approached the landing zone a few dozen meters away from the summit. The pilots and the commandos could suddenly make out footprints and signs of human activity on the snow. "*The LZ is hot, abort mission!*" But it is already too late, several RPGs are fired at the MH-47E, while the chunky 14,5 mm

Although this picture was not taken during Operation *Anaconda*, it illustrates quite well the mountainous operating conditions along the valley of Shah-e-Kot. Helicopters were used for troop insertion and extraction, resupply and proved once more that they were invaluable in that sort of terrain. On the other hand, when landing, like in Takur Ghar, these aircraft were easy prey for the Taliban.
(DOD Photo)

OPERATION "ANACONDA"

heavy machine gun shells go clean through the fuselage and wound a crew member. The hydraulic systems are soon shot to pieces, the damaged helicopter leaks gallons of oil that quickly turn the cargo hold into one very slippery mess. The pilot struggled with his controls to try and fly his badly mauled helicopter out of this inferno; the MH47E bucked and almost rolled out of control. Unfortunately, at this very moment, US Navy SEAL NEIL ROBERTS is on the back ramp of the helicopter. Losing his balance and slipping on the oil-covered deck of the Chinook, he fell in the snow a few meters below. He was then alone, in the dark of a very early morning, facing a group off "Al-Qaida" members with nothing but his Minimi light machine gun. A few minutes later, seven kilometres away from Takur Ghar, Razor 03 finally came to a controlled crash.

The fate of Petty Officer First Class Neil Roberts is not clear. What seems to be sure is that he managed to keep his enemies at bay with his M249 SAW (Squad Automatic Weapon), until he ran out of ammunition; he was then finished off.

At the same time, on board Razor 03 the team had realized that their comrade had disappeared and the CCT managed to contact an AC-130 to provide "top cover" for the missing SEAL: but it was already too late, the thermal sights of the "Gunship" only managing to track down the SEAL when he already was surrounded by four or five individuals. Some minutes later, Razor 04 which has just dropped its own team landed close to the wreck of Razor 03 and extracted the crew and the SF operators before heading back to Gardez. As soon as they landed there the five SEALs and the CCT decided, in agreement with the Razor 04 crew to return to the spot where Roberts had fallen to try and save him. They knew their only option was to brave the gauntlet of "Al-Qaida's" fire once more by landing on the same LZ (Landing Zone) because no others were available; walking from the bottom of the valley to the summit was not an option since it would take a minimum of three hours and time was already running very short.

Finally, it was 5AM when Razor 04 returned to the LZ. "Al-Qaida's" fire was even fiercer than on the first try and the gunmen just could not miss the enormous target provided by the twin-rotored helicopter. Howe-

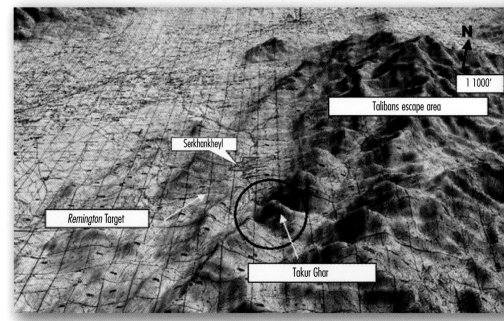

Talibans escape area

1 1000'

Serkhankheyl

Remington Target

Takur Ghar

ver, the six members of the commando managed to jump out of the MH-47E unscathed and to get into effective defensive positions. Even though hit by several rounds, the helicopter also managed to limp back to its base. The US operators used their superior training and their night vision goggles to good use; they moved swiftly towards the summit that they identified thanks to a lone tree and a cliff that were silhouetted against the early morning sky. While progressing towards these specific ground features, the CCT, Technical Sergeant Chapman, spotted two enemy hidden under the tree. Chapman and the SEAL closer to him fired two bursts of their M-4s and suppressed those two "hostiles". But in doing so, they failed to identify another enemy position located less than twenty metres from them and which had so far remained silent. The first AK burst from this position hit the CCT who collapsed; the SEA-

L's reaction was immediate: they opened up with all their weapons an threw several grenades at the enemy bunker. But to no avail! The "A Qaida" fighters were tough and they fought for every inch of this for gotten summit, wounding another two SEALs in the process. Being inc pable of moving ahead any more in the face of such a strong opposition the SEALs decided to bring their wounded team mates back to the L under the protection of an AC-130 that they had just contacted. Durin their retreat, they managed to kill another two enemy.

While these gun battles were raging on, two MH-47E helicopters, ca signs Razor 01 and Razor 02, loaded with, in the first chopper, a grou of ten Rangers, a Tactical Air Controller (TACP), a USAF Combat Contro ler (CCT) and a USAF Pararescueman (PJ), and in the second, ten oth Rangers, were heading at full speed towards Takur Ghar. These tw

It was now 5.45 AM, the sun was only just starting to warm the desolate mountaintop when Razor 01 and Razor 02 approached the LZ on a southern course. The "Al-Qaida" fighters, who had already killed two Americans, heard the rotor noise and got ready for yet another American heliborne insertion.

As soon as it neared the LZ, Razor 01 was almost immediately hit by an RPG7 on its right-hand side; then all hell broke loose, rounds of all calibres impacting on the Chinook's fuselage. The pilot desperately tried to gain some altitude, but the MH-47E, already stricken to death, crashed to the ground. Fortunately, the helicopter came to rest on a thick snowdrift that somewhat cushioned the impact with the ground. While all this was happening, Sergeant Phil Svitak, the door gunner of Razor 01 had had time to open fire with his machine-gun but this did not last long as the withering fire soon hit him too; he died within seconds.

Inside the downed chopper, a certain state of shock settled for a few moments as the blood of the door gunner spluttered on the survivors; to make matter even worse, SPC Marc Anderson was then hit and killed outright. In spite of the incredible volume of fire that was thrown at them by the Islamist volunteers who seemed to have an inextinguishable stock of ammunition, the Rangers still managed to extricate them-

selves from the cargo compartment of the Chinook. At the front of the aircraft, the two seriously wounded pilots remained stuck in their cockpit that was unfortunately positioned just opposite one of Ben Laden's gunmen's bunker! During the ensuing exchanges of fire, Sergeant Brad Crose and Corporal Matt Commons also got also killed.

Ignoring the bullets that were whizzing around him, Pararescueman Senior Airman Jason Cunningham, began to treat the numerous wounded Rangers who were now suffering in silence. At the same time, a Ranger Fire Team leader decided to counter-attack in order to reach better fighting positions. While running and dodging bullets, he still managed to shoot and kill two enemy gunmen with his M-4, including an RPG gunner. This feat in itself speaks volume for the quality of Ranger training. After a first assault which failed to drive the Taliban back from their positions, the Rangers realized that their opponents were too numerous to be defeated by the QRF; they then asked their USAF CCT to contact the air coordination centre for some "*very close*" support. Less than three minutes later, F/A-18s started their strafing runs on the positions of the Islamist fighters, dropping their 500 lbs bombs less than fifty metres from the stranded US soldiers!

It was then 7AM, and their opponents could no longer overrun the

bove. Helicopters played a vital role during this war. These are soldiers from the 82nd Airborne protecting the unloading of ases of medicine for the inhabitants of Shumace, a village located in e southern mountains of Afghanistan. In the foreground, on the left, ote an American Special Forces soldier protecting the paras and the elicopter from a potential Taliban attack. (*DOD Picture*)

Above right. Photo taken about ten days after the fighting. In the meanwhile the snow has melted. However in the center f the picture notice the wrecked Razor I helicopter, too badly damaged to be able to fly. Much later a Russian heavy-lift helicopter came and lifted it off to Bagram. (*DOD Picture*)

pposite left. Presenting the position on Takur Ghar during Operation naconda. (*MOD Document*)

Opposite right. Coalition forces were to undertake identical operations several times in the same zones to hunt the groups of Talibans who regularly came back to the same spots. Special Forces and Kabul government soldiers can be seen here progressing in the zone around Tora Bora during Operation Torii in May, 2002. (*DOD Picture*)

ams were the QRF (Quick Reaction Force) whose normal mission is to e permanently ready to answer within fifteen minutes the sort of emer- ency situation the SEALs were currently experiencing on the top of their olated mountain. However, when the QRF took off from its base, infor- ation on the SEAL's predicament was at best very sketchy and radio ntact with the isolated navy commandos was reduced to a barely audi- e gabble. When the SEALs had begun their descent, the US Command ad approved their request for assistance and it had dispatched the QRF its two helicopters. Regrettably, the commander of the QRF aboard azor 01 never received the updated orders that stated the new coor- nates of the SEALs. As a consequence, the Rangers headed straight r the original LZ, where Razor 03 and 04 had taken so much ground re and where the SEALs no longer were.

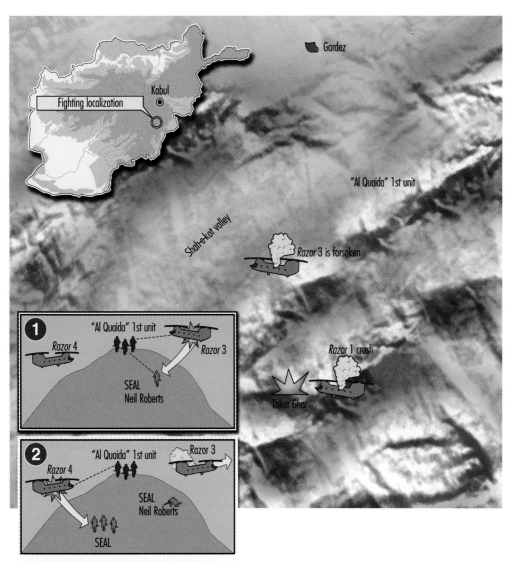

Gardez

Fighting localization

Kabul

"Al Quaida" 1st unit

Shah-e-kot valley

Razor 3 is forsaken

Razor 1 crash

Takur Ghar

1
"Al Quaida" 1st unit
Razor 4 — Razor 3
SEAL Neil Roberts

2
"Al Quaida" 1st unit
Razor 4 — Razor 3
SEAL Neil Roberts
SEAL

3
"Al Quaida" 1st unit
Razor 4 — Razor 1
SEAL Neil Roberts
SEAL

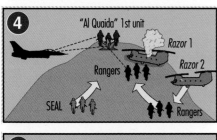

4
"Al Quaida" 1st unit
Razor 1
Razor 2
Rangers
SEAL
Rangers

5
SEAL + Rangers
Razor 1
Blessés
"Al Quaida" 2nd unit

6
Razor 1
Helicopters from 160th SOAR

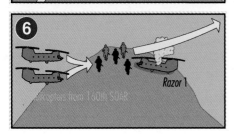

Rangers.

While Razor 01 was being shot to pieces, Razor 02 landed on a safe spot and waited for a fragmentary order that would cover the new situation that they were now obviously facing. The commander of this element then decided to drop ten Rangers accompanied by one SEAL, one thousand metres below the summit, in order to try and establish some sort of liaison with the SEALs of Razor 03. Once the liaison was established, the Rangers were ordered to climb towards the summit. This they achieved in two hours, under continuous mortar fire, in deep snow, loaded with all their weapons and combat gear on a hillside which incline varied between 45 ° in 70 °. At 1030 AM, totally exhausted, they reached their surrounded comrades in front of the enemy positions. I was now time for the Rangers to assault the Taliban's position, but before they actually could get to them they had to go across a 50 metre long flat piece of ground that afforded absolutely no cover from enemy fire whatsoever. To make this crossing less suicidal, the USAF CC called in air support and, when the smoke began to clear, seven Rangers, supported by two machine guns, dashed for the summit as fast as their weary legs would carry them, knee deep in snow, firing short bursts of their M-4s, lobbing M-203 rounds and throwing hand grenades. I two minutes of savage close-quarters fighting, the enemy bunkers were cleared and their defenders killed.

The Rangers then lost no time and reinforced their positions. The commanders' estimate was that their position was now easier to defend and that the wounded were going to be safer there than around the wreck of the helicopter. In those conditions, it took a minimum of four to six stretcher bearers to take just one wounded from the helicopter wreck to the summit; a considerable effort by all accounts, but it also had to be undertaken under the fire of the remaining "Al-Qaida" gunmen who, from a nearby summit less than four hundred meters away, began to shoot at the bearers and at their wounded charges.

Immediately, the Rangers and the CCTs put the WIA (Wounded In Action) under cover and fired back with their M-203 grenade launcher. Realizing quickly that those 40 mm grenades were not going to be sufficient to suppress the Taliban's fire the CCTs then called air power to the rescue once again. In just two passes, American aircrafts destroyed the enemy positions. Sadly, around the same time, Senior Airman Jason Cunningham, who had been the first Pararescueman to be wounded in this operation died in the arms of his comrades.

Once the Rangers had all regrouped, they strengthened their positions; they collected the wounded and the dead on the summit and started to wait for the night for a helicopter extraction. They knew that the

Belove.
Soldiers from the 82nd Airborne and American Special Forces climb aboard a Chinook to be taken to the southeastern part of Afghanistan, near Pakistan. The unsuccessful operations around Tora Bora in December 2001 allowed many « Al-Qaida » fighters to slip into Pakistan.
(DOD Picture)

66

Above.
A view of the combat zone the following morning as the American fighter-bombers continue to "pound" suspected positions of the Talibans and their allies.
(DOD Picture)

Below.
During the summer of 2002, Canadian soldiers from the 3rd PPCLI have a hard time progressing through the rugged terrain north of Qualat. Accompanied by Special Forces, they are part of Operation Cherokee Sky with the assigned objective of finding and destroying the last Talibans left in the area. It is certain that the defeat of the Talibans and their « Al-Qaida » allies during Operation Anaconda led them to desert many areas and seek refuge in tribal regions of Pakistan.
(DOD Picture)

Above.
During Operation Snipe in May, 2002, British recce teams from Task Force Jacana discover important ammunition caches and destroy them. On the top of Takur Ghar in March, 2002, the American Special Forces didn't expect to find so much resistance and such motivated fighters. *(MOD Picture)*

chances of a daytime extraction were very slim since "Al-Qaida's" members were still lobbing mortar rounds and firing with sniper rifles at the Ranger's positions.

At the same time, in order to relieve the pressure on the isolated group of American soldiers, several OPs (Observation Posts) were established by American Special Forces and Australian SAS on neighbouring hills in order to guide in attack aircrafts against "Al-Qaida's" elements that were trying to launch attacks in the direction of the Takur Ghar summit.

At 20.15, four helicopters of the 160th Special Operations Aviation Regiment (SOAR) managed to extract the Rangers from their summit and the SEALs from their mountain hillsides. Two hours later, the survivors landed on Bagram air base. In the morning, the eleven WIAs arrived in military hospitals in Germany.

Operation Anaconda lasted for another nineteen days before "Al-Qaida's" last elements were flushed from the Shah-e-Kot valley.

THE RANGERS JUMP OVER AFGHANISTAN

Above.
On July 16th 2002, on the Kandahar airstrip,
a group of US Army Rangers board a USAF C-17 Globemaster III
bound for the Bagram US Special Forces camp.
(USAF Picture)

Thirteen days after the beginning of air bombardments against various Taliban military infrastructures, the American command decided to launch two separate operations against targets located in the South of Afghanistan; one operation was to be heliborne and the other airborne.

The purpose of those operations was almost as political and psychological as it was military. They were mostly meant to show the Taliban and their allies that the American could now strike where and when they chose to. The hidden agenda behind those operations was a massive deception operation aiming to draw the world's attention on a "*dog and pony show*" while, at the same time, in the North of the country, about ten detachments of special forces were linking up and training Northern Alliance units.

The first combat jump
since Panama

CENTCOM chose to wrap two operations into one. One was to be a classic operation and the other an antiterrorist operation. The classic operation was to be an airborne operation in

which the Rangers were to play the main role. That sort of short duration raid is no novelty for the Ranger Battalions that train and specialize in that type of action, especially the seizure of airport terminals like they did in Grenada in 1983 and in Panama in 1989.

The 75th Rangers Regiment is made up of three battalions that rotate in the high-readiness, pre-readiness and training roles. The 3rd Ranger Battalion was the first to be deployed in Afghanistan and it was followed by the 1st from December, 2001).

Rangers of the 3rd battalion embarked at the beginning of October, flew to Oman in the Persian Gulf and were ready to be deployed on the ground by October 7. The green light was given ten days later but before being actually deployed, various operations had to be coordinated and the weather conditions of Afghanistan had to be carefully considered.

On October 19, at 22.00, under the command of Colonel Joseph L. Votel, some 100 Rangers of the 3rd battalion who had been flown in from Oman in MC-130 Hercules were parachuted in the vicinity of a dirt strip near Bolangi, about a hundred kilometres South of Kandahar. This track was to become famous a month later, when, under the name of Camp Rhino,

it became a Marine Corps advanced base. It is interesting to note that those Rangers only did their very low altitude combat jump after Army Pathfinders had jumped in first, done a reconnaissance of the area, cleared it and marked it for the mass jump and secured it. This is a good illustration of the usual squabbles between Rangers and Special Forces, the latter being considered as "week end paratroopers" by the former who insisted that this combat jump had to be trusted to "*real*" paratroopers.

While the jump took place, Rangers John J. Edmunds and Kristofor T. Stonesifer of the 3rd Battalion who were riding in one of the CSAR (Combat Search And Rescue) helicopter which had been allocated to this mission were killed when their UH-60 Blackhawk crashed in Pakistan.

Once on the ground, the Rangers regrouped, tended to the thirty slightly injured soldiers the jump had caused (sprains, and

68

Ranger in Kandahar, December 2001
The Minimi is the normal Ranger Battalion's Squad Automatic Weapon(SAW); it is light, versatile but it packs a heavy punch in the form of its 200, 100 or 30 5,56mm rounds magazines. An M9 pistol (Beretta 92F) is the regulation secondary weapon for this SAW gunner. He is dressed in the three-colours desert BDU and sports knee pads and Bollé XT-800 goggles fitted on to the Kevlar helmet which was worn at all time in spite of its weight. His load bearing equipment is the MOLLE II which has been here favoured over the MOLLE RACK system. The rest of the equipment is carried in a Blackhawk non regulation patrol pack.

69

Above.
On an air base in Oman,
Rangers from the 3rd Battalion board
an MC-130E Hercules a few hours before
doing a combat jump on the Bolangi airstrip
South of Kandahar. It was the Ranger's first
combat jump since Panama in 1989.
(DOD Picture)

**Ranger belonging to one of the light
and very mobile 75th Ranger Regiment
Recon Teams.**
Wearing the three-colours desert BDU, he has pulled
a woodland camouflage anorak on top of his BDU jacket
in order to blend more efficiently with his surrounding
in an often seen combination. This reconstructed figure still uses
the old LC-2 LBE that were still to be seen among the more
modern TLBV and LCV MOLLE some Rangers disliked.
The uniform is completed by a pair of the ever-popular Nomex
aviator gloves and the local Pakol Afghan hat which protects
from the cold and contributes to the camouflage
of this Ranger. The pouch for the M-40 gas mask hanging
from his belt reveals that this operator is most certainly
engaged in some cave clearing operations during which
CS gas were used. The M-4 rifle is fitted with the RIS system
as well as an AN/PEQ-2 laser pointer, an M-68 Aimpoint
sight and a tactical torch.

Above.
"Stand up, Hook up ! " on the 19th of October 2001, aboard an MC-130, Rangers from the 3rd Battalion get ready for a low-level jump over Bolangi.
(DOD Picture)

**Ranger during Operation *Appolo*
in Zhawar Kili.**

At the beginning of 2002, the Zhawar Kili area was the scene of intense anti-Taliban and "Al Qaida" operations. As seen in this reconstruction of a Ranger, for those short-duration operations, the Rangers tended to use only light equipment; three-colours desert BDU, mountain boots instead of the regulation Altama desert boots, a Shemagh and the RACK (Ranger Assault Carrying Kit, based on the MOLLE system) as load bearing equipment. An M9 pistol is carried in a low slung tactical holster and the main weapon is the ubiquitous M4/M203 "over-under" combination.

ther) and secured the area but they soon realized ne zone they had been allocated was completely empty. The irt track and the forlorn buildings which had been built for rich rabs from the Gulf who wanted to practise falcon hunting in he region were all deserted. After having held the area for everal hours, a stream of Blackhawk and Chinook helicopters elonging to the 160th Special Operations Aviation Regiment ame to extract the Rangers and flew them to several discreet ir bases in Pakistan.

As these events were unfolding, another heliborne operation vas launched some kilometres from Kandahar, the Taliban fief- om, against a series of buildings that were supposed to be ear- narked to shelter Mullah Omar in case of needs.

This operation was mostly left to Delta Force; its mission was to eliminate the sentinels, to "*take down*" the building, to search them thoroughly and to capture the greatest possible number of Taliban and documents. Mullah Omar was not present, but it was still thought that the seized documents were worth it and that the psychological impact had been very important on the enemies. That operation cost the American the accidental loss of two helicopters.

In the heart of Anaconda

Following the airborne operation, the Rangers remained based in Pakistan and in Oman. Several other operations were planned, but the speed of the Northern Alliance advance was such they all had to be cancelled. On November 23, 2001, some two hundred 3rd Battalion Rangers carrying with them all their equipment including Tactical Laser Designators and some green Berets of the 5th SFG flew back to the USA from the Jacobabad Pakistani air base in C-130 via Turkey. For them, the Afghan campaign was over.

1ST RANGER BN

RANGER AIRBORNE
2D BN 75TH INF

3D RANGER BN

...evious page, left:

...OUT (Military Operations in Urban Terrain) exercises
...ndertaken by a Ranger from the 75th Rangers Regiment.
...mong the main missions of this regiment are the seizure
...airports (a mission successfully achieved in Grenada in 1983
...nd in Panama in 1989) and quick hit-and-run raids for which
...ey are well trained and equipped. In Afghanistan, the Rangers
...uickly adapted to other missions like the clearing
...tunnel complexes in mountainous areas.
...USASOC Picture)

Top, from left to right:
public relation pictures showing some of the various skills
mastered by the Rangers, namely Close Quarter Battle
using light weapons, "heavy" support weapons
with an M224 60 mm mortar and reconnaissance
missions on an armed RSOV
(Rangers Special Operations Vehicle).
(75th Ranger Regiment Pictures)

Ranger during Operation Condor, 2002

...rting on May 16, 2002 the Fort Lewis 2nd
...allion took over. The Rangers participated
...Operations Condor and Buzzard, combing the
...untryside in the mountainous zones southeast
...Kandahar. The weather is relatively mild,
...the clothing is lightweight. The Camelback is
...nust, easily adapted to the MOLLE jacket.
...s soldier is carrying a rope harness for rappelling
...crossing difficult terrain.

...MOLLE jacket is fitted out for a SAW gunner. Two
...ckets for 200-round ammunition boxes,
...o pockets for 100-round cloth pouches, four
...kets for M16-style magazines to be used
...h the Minimi. His M-249 SAW is the "para"
...sion with a short barrel and telescopic butt,
...ier to use in this type of terrain.

A Ranger from the 3rd Batallion of the 75th Ranger
Regiment during a night jump, on October 20, 2001, south of
Kandahar. His basic outfit includes the BDU fatigues in the three-colored
"desert" camouflage version, adopted during the Gulf War in 1991.
For protection from the cold, he is wearing an M65 Field Jacket with
the same camouflage pattern. His "Fritz" Kevlar helmet has a "desert"
helmet cover where the ranger has placed his Bollé XT800 goggles
designed for balistics protection. He has an LC2 harness, often replaced
by MOLLE I or II modular jackets, with Y suspenders in the back, where
he has attached two magazine carriers, a one-liter water bottle, an Alice
pack, a three-part folding shovel and an M9 bayonnette. He is carrying
his SDU-5/E Strobe Light in a case attached to his left harness strap. In
an M12 Bianchi holster, a Beretta M9 to be used as a back-up
weapon, the main one being the 5.56-mm M-4 Colt rifle equiped with
a 40-mm M203 grenade launcher. He has an M17A1 or M40 gas
mask tied to his belt. For his personal protection he is wearing Nomex
pilots gloves, an excellent
compromise between the
need for insulation and
for preserving a sense
of touch. He has Kevlar-
lined leather gloves
hanging from the hip ring
of his gas mask bag. They
will be used for body searches
of suspects arrested in the
zone around Helmand,
during "Al-Qaida" search
missions. His attire also
includes
Blackhawk
knee pads.

A Ranger during *Operation Mountain Sweep*.
At the end of September 2002, the Rangers, alongside
the 82nd Airborne Division, took part in Operation *Mountain
Sweep* which ended with the capture of 11 suspects
including two with foreign passports but missed the "Al Qaida" finance expert
it was targeting. The length of this operation was such that Rangers
who normally "travel light" had to carry heavy loads,
(here a non regulation Blackhawk rucksacks) as well as
some warm clothing like the old M65 Field Jacket.
The weapon is a camouflaged M-4 fitted with the RIS system
and AN/PEQ-2 laser pointer and he also carries some "frags" (hand grenades)
on his belt for immediate use in the tunnel complexes.

The weapons and equipments of a Rangers battalion

Each Ranger rifleman is issued with a 5, 56 mm M-4 rifle and AT-4 disposable anti-tank rockets. Each battalion also fields 54 SAW M249 5,56 mm light machine guns, 27 M240G 7,62mm machine guns, 12 MK-19 40mm automatic grenade launchers, 16 RAW 84 mm recoilless rifles, 12 Browning M2 12,7mm heavy machine guns , 6 M224 60 mm mortars and 12 Javelin missiles.

The only vehicles on the Rangers' list of equipments are its 12 RSOV (Ranger Special Operations

Vehicle), which are modified Land Rover armed with M240Gs, MK-19s, or M2 machine guns; one crew member is also equipped with an antitank weapon (RAWS, AT-4, Law or Javelin). Apart from the RSOV, ten modified Kawasaki 250 cc motorcycles called Ranger Special Operations Motorcycle (RSOM) are also authorized to each battalion.

On December 7, 2001 in the morning, 200 Rangers of the 3rd Battalion returned to their Fort Benning barracks. They left mild Afghan temperatures for the freezing cold. "*That's what happens in Fort Benning, the fog rises and the best soldiers in the world arrive!*" said General Paul Eaton, commander of the 75th Rangers Regiment, in a welcome home speech that did not last more than 30 seconds because of the bitter cold.

At the beginning of January, 2002, the 3rd battalion was replaced by the 1st battalion which is normally based in Georgia; it was immediately placed under Special Forces command in Bagram. On January 24, several Ranger platoons took part in operations launched against "Al-Qaida" training camps that were still suspected of harbouring members of this organization. After those operations, the Rangers were involved in *Operation Apollo* which saw the discovery and the clearing up of several tunnels and cave networks in the Zhawar Kili region.

On March the 1st began the most important American operation in Afghanistan known to date, *Operation Anaconda.* Four days later, three Rangers of the 1st battalion met their death during the very fierce Takur Ghar fighting. (See boxed text on this page). The Rangers who paid the ultimate price were Sergeant Bradley S. Crose, Corporal Matthew Commonds and Specialist Marc Anderson. They died trying to rescue a US Navy SEAL who had fallen from an MH-47 Chinook in front of "Al-Qaida" positions. They were posthumously awarded the Bronze Star, the Purple Heart and the Medal of the Merit. Rangers were supposed to exit their helicopter from the back ramp as they had done a hundred times in training before; "*But, all hell broke loose when enemy rounds began to drill the cabin like a hot knife through butter*" recalled the medical specialist who was also on board the helicopter; "*the first Ranger was killed before he had time to move and the two others while they were running towards the back cargo door*" The survivors then dove into the snow looking for any protection against the enemy fire which was coming from well prepared and reinforced positions overhanging the wreck of Chinook. "*I saw one of the gunmen shooting at me*" recalled Staff Sergeant Raymond DePouli "*I could see tracers coming my way and a shrapnel hit my body armour; I emptied my magazine into him and that quietened him definitively*"

At the same time, three RPGs hit the wrecked Chinook, killing and wounding other Americans who were still trapped inside. Protected by big boulders, the Rangers threw several grenades at their enemies but the range was too great and they did not achieve the desired effect. The only solution then seemed to be a frontal assault. The Rangers leaped and darted, stopping less than 30 metres from the "Al-Qaida" position to evaluate them before the final assault It came after a series of USAF F-15 and F-16 bombardments. All the survivors agreed on the fact that years of drill and rehearsal really had saved the day because endless practise had taught them how to react in a fire fight and how to use their weapons efficiently under stress.

Beautiful revenge on the Somalia tragedy

After three months of deployment in Afghanistan, some 200 Rangers of the 1st Battalion returned to their Hunter Army Airfield barracks on April 12, 2002. They were replaced by their brothers-in-arms of the 2nd battalion based in Fort Lewis. After *Operation Anaconda,* Rangers participated in *Operation Condor* from the May 16, then *operation Buzzard* on May 28. On August 8, several Rangers platoons were also deployed during *Operation Mountain Lion* and *Operation Mountain Sweep*. Mountain Sweep was the most important operation since *Anaconda* in March 2002, and it involved 1 000 American soldiers from the 82nd Airborne division, Rangers and US Navy SEALs. Special Forces teams managed to arrest eleven suspects, two of whom possessing occidental passports, but a more important target, an "Al-Qaida" finance expert managed to escape unscathed.

Those various operations all amounted to a very sweet revenge for the Rangers who had lost eighteen of their comrades in the streets of Mogadishu nine years before.

Top left: In Fort Bragg, on November the 21st 2001, Defence Secretary Donald Rumsfeld is introduced to some Ranger weaponry after a presentation of the capabilities of a Ranger Battalion. *(DOD Picture)*

Bottom picture: a Ranger operating alongside 82nd Airborne Division paratroopers in an hostile area films an house search operation. Rangers have been present in Afghanistan since the beginning of operations there in 2001. *(75th Ranger Regiment Picture)*

If American military operations in Afghanistan did not genera
major battles or any really stiff resistance, the American propagan
machine, on the other hand, was used on a massive scale. Psycho
gical operations were first used in a very unsophisticated way by t
Taliban and "Al-Qaida" members, but they were quickly eliminate
from the propaganda game by the American units specialized in psych
logical operations.

The American armed forces deployed several PsyOps teams at t
sharp end of operations in order to get their propaganda messa
across to the gunmen of the different armed groups as well as to rea
the civilian population that would inevitably get caught at some poi
in the crossfire. Radio broadcasts and pamphlet droppings were us
on a grand scale to reach even the remotest parts of the country.

The first Psyops operation was launched at the beginning of Oc
ber, 2001. Its purpose was to produce several news programmes
Dari and Pachtoun that were then broadcast from a USAFSOC EC-13
Commando Solo, which operated from Oman. The Department
Defence called those American programmes "news broadcast", a
they served their tactical purposes well - indeed, messages warned t
Afghan population to get away from military installations, official bu

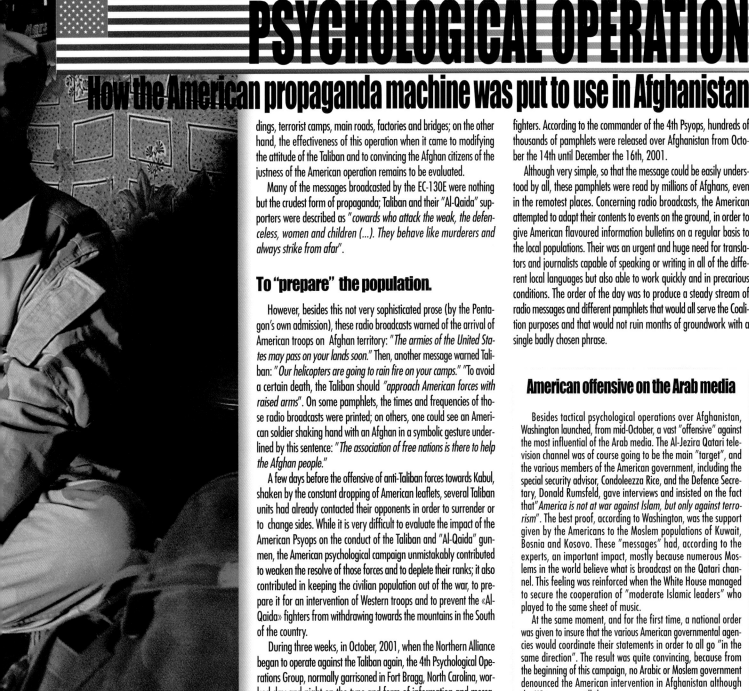

PSYCHOLOGICAL OPERATION
How the American propaganda machine was put to use in Afghanistan

dings, terrorist camps, main roads, factories and bridges; on the other hand, the effectiveness of this operation when it came to modifying the attitude of the Taliban and to convincing the Afghan citizens of the justness of the American operation remains to be evaluated.

Many of the messages broadcasted by the EC-130E were nothing but the crudest form of propaganda; Taliban and their "Al-Qaida" supporters were described as "*cowards who attack the weak, the defenceless, women and children (...). They behave like murderers and always strike from afar*".

To "prepare" the population.

However, besides this not very sophisticated prose (by the Pentagon's own admission), these radio broadcasts warned of the arrival of American troops on Afghan territory: "*The armies of the United States may pass on your lands soon.*" Then, another message warned Taliban: "*Our helicopters are going to rain fire on your camps.*" "To avoid a certain death, the Taliban should "*approach American forces with raised arms*". On some pamphlets, the times and frequencies of those radio broadcasts were printed; on others, one could see an American soldier shaking hand with an Afghan in a symbolic gesture underlined by this sentence: "*The association of free nations is there to help the Afghan people.*"

A few days before the offensive of anti-Taliban forces towards Kabul, shaken by the constant dropping of American leaflets, several Taliban units had already contacted their opponents in order to surrender or to change sides. While it is very difficult to evaluate the impact of the American Psyops on the conduct of the Taliban and "Al-Qaida" gunmen, the American psychological campaign unmistakably contributed to weaken the resolve of those forces and to deplete their ranks; it also contributed in keeping the civilian population out of the war, to prepare it for an intervention of Western troops and to prevent the «Al-Qaida» fighters from withdrawing towards the mountains in the South of the country.

During three weeks, in October, 2001, when the Northern Alliance began to operate against the Taliban again, the 4th Psychological Operations Group, normally garrisoned in Fort Bragg, North Carolina, worked day and night on the type and form of information and messages that should be used on the Afghan population and on the Afghan

fighters. According to the commander of the 4th Psyops, hundreds of thousands of pamphlets were released over Afghanistan from October the 14th until December the 16th, 2001.

Although very simple, so that the message could be easily understood by all, these pamphlets were read by millions of Afghans, even in the remotest places. Concerning radio broadcasts, the American attempted to adapt their contents to events on the ground, in order to give American flavoured information bulletins on a regular basis to the local populations. Their was an urgent and huge need for translators and journalists capable of speaking or writing in all of the different local languages but also able to work quickly and in precarious conditions. The order of the day was to produce a steady stream of radio messages and different pamphlets that would all serve the Coalition purposes and that would not ruin months of groundwork with a single badly chosen phrase.

American offensive on the Arab media

Besides tactical psychological operations over Afghanistan, Washington launched, from mid-October, a vast "offensive" against the most influential of the Arab media. The Al-Jezira Qatari television channel was of course going to be the main "target", and the various members of the American government, including the special security advisor, Condoleezza Rice, and the Defence Secretary, Donald Rumsfeld, gave interviews and insisted on the fact that "*America is not at war against Islam, but only against terrorism*". The best proof, according to Washington, was the support given by the Americans to the Moslem populations of Kuwait, Bosnia and Kosovo. These "messages" had, according to the experts, an important impact, mostly because numerous Moslems in the world believe what is broadcast on the Qatari channel. This feeling was reinforced when the White House managed to secure the cooperation of "moderate Islamic leaders" who played to the same sheet of music.

At the same moment, and for the first time, a national order was given to insure that the various American governmental agencies would coordinate their statements in order to all go "in the same direction". The result was quite convincing, because from the beginning of this campaign, no Arabic or Moslem government denounced the American intervention in Afghanistan although the US troop are still there.

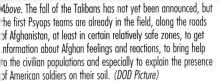

Above. The fall of the Talibans has not yet been announced, but the first Psyops teams are already in the field, along the roads of Afghanistan, at least in certain relatively safe zones, to get information about Afghan feelings and reactions, to bring help to the civilian populations and especially to explain the presence of American soldiers on their soil. *(DOD Picture)*

Left. Escorted by soldiers of the 3rd Platoon, 101st Military Police Company from Fort Campbell Kentucky, a Psyops team of TPT 913 visits the neighbouring villages to inform villagers on the objectives of the American armed forces and to collect information. The mission of the Psyops is also to try and earn the confidence of the population by inquiring on its vital needs, such as care for the youth or children's education. In those situations, matters relevant to children and women must, of course, be dealt with through the village's elders. *(DOD Picture)*

Opposite right.
In the Salog district, on December 19, 2002, two A-Company sergeants from the 9th Psychological Operations Battalion distribute brochures published by their unit for the Afghans. This is taking place while other soldiers from the 405th Civil Affairs Battalion repair the district school and carry out humanitarian assistance. *(DOD Picture)*

Leaflet Number: AFD94

YOU ARE TRAPPE

Taliban and Al Qaida Fighters
We know where
You are hiding

Al-Qai'da do you think that you are safe...

توقف!
از اینجا دور شوید!
د دی ځای نه لری شی!

TALIBAN/AL QAIDA FIGHTERS:
YOU ARE OUR TARGETS!

AFGHANISTAN=PEACE PROSPERIT

A NEW
GOVERNMEN
OFFERS NE
FREEDOMS

Leaflet Number: AF5-C-11-HB1

A UNITED AFGHANISTAN=PEACE PROSPERITY

THE FUTURE OF
AFGHANISTAN DEPENDS
ON YOUR SUPPORT OF
THE NEW GOVERNMENT

A NEW
GOVERNMENT
OFFERS NEW
FREEDOMS

Leaflet Number: AFG08

RE OF
STAN DEPENDS
ON YOUR SUPPORT OF
THE NEW GOVERNMENT

Leaflet Number: AFG09

78

"They dishonoured Afghanistan…"

The Pentagon released several million pamphlets and broadcasted dozens of hours of radio messages in two languages, during more than three weeks.

Among all the messages, two were privileged: *"We ask you, you the true Afghan people, to bring to justice Ussama Ben Laden and the members of his terrorist group for crimes committed against an innocent people";*

"Not only did Ussama Ben Laden and the "Al-Qaida" terrorist group committed crimes against the United States, but they also dishonoured Afghanistan and they continue to cause war in your country.

They use your country as base for terrorism to kill your people and innocent Americans. These terrorists tarnish the reputation of the Afghan people and of Islam."

Previous page : a few examples among many others of leaflets prepared and produced by psyops units and dropped by USAFSOC aircrafts. Those leaflets were to be understandable by all and they aimed at depriving the terrorist movements of their popular support. *(DOD Picture)*

This page, from top to bottom: Air Force Senior Master Sergeant Marlin Haldeman, crewmember of a 193rd Special Operation Wing EC-130E Commando Solo doing a series of pre-broadcast checks before going "on-air". According to the Pentagon, at least one EC-130E Commando Solo was flying around-the-clock over or around Afghanistan during the campaign, broadcasting news and information for the benefit of the Afghan population. Those 193rd Special Operation Wing aircrafts of the Pennsylvania Air National Guard are normally based in Harrisburgh, Pa and they broadcast the messages prepared by the 4th Psychological Operations Group in the different languages relevant to their area of deployment. After their successful deployment over Iraq in 1991, the EC-130E Commando Solo were also deployed in Haiti, Somalia and in Iraq again in 2003.

Day and night, at high altitude or low altitude, the EC-130E Commando Solo was orbiting… USAF Chief Master Sergeant James Bankes of the 193rd Special Operation Wing of the Pennsylvania Air National Guard monitors the quality of TV images that are being broadcasted to a foreign audience. Since Taliban law forbade any sort of TV broadcast, Psyops were limited to radios during the Afghan campaign.

The EC-130E Commando Solo is an extensively modified, C-130 Hercules. It is fitted with all the necessary equipment to broadcast TV and radio programmes on areas designated by the US commander that has it under its control. Each unit costs 70 million USD and needs an 11-man crew to man all of its workstations. *(USAF Pictures)*

PSYCHOLOGICAL OPERATIONS

Psychological operations are considered by the American government as vital part of political, military, economic and ideological operations.

PSYOPS units (Psychological Operations units) are in charge of broadcasting information to foreign audiences in support of American policies and national objectives around the world.

Undertaken in peacetime and war, these actions are not classified as "offensives", because they use non-violent technique albeit in a violent environment. The ultimate objective of these units is to convince the enemy, the non-belligerent and the friendly populations to side with the United States and their allies.

Psychological operations are undertaken on the long term and at the tactical, theatre and strategic levels and they target vast audiences or key players. At the theatre level, PSYOPS are used by the commander to directly act on his battleground; at the tactical level, the range of those operations will be even more limited and they will specifically aim at faster action in order to break the morale and the combat efficiency of the opponent. Besides strictly military operations, PSYOPS can also work in association with other American governmental agencies, during humanitarian relief operations for example, or during anti-narcotics operations. These activities aim to pass on information about ready-made programs and to attract the support of the population.

As of now, the Civil Affairs units of the US Army operate according to geographical zones, languages and to the cultural knowledge and backgrounds of their soldiers. The 4th Psychological Operations Group (Airborne) based in Fort Bragg, North Carolina is the only active duty unit of this kind in the US Army. Its manpower is made up of 26% of active-duty soldiers but the remaining 74 % are divided between the 2nd and the 7th PSYOPS groups that belong to the Army Reserve.

Right, from top to bottom.
Meeting with the Haqdad Kelay village council, where they explained the purposes and the missions of the American armed forces against Taliban and "Al-Qaida" fighters, Psyops and their escorts get back to their loudspeakers equipped Humvees. During the offensive part of the operations, the Afghan populations received massive pamphlets and food rations airdrops, and were subjected to intensive radio broadcasts coupled with the action of Psyops teams on the ground. This campaign has witnessed some exemplary psychological operations, all led in a difficult country that has been savaged by twenty years of continuous wars.

A soldier belonging to Tactical Psychological Operations Team (TPT) 913 of Fort Bragg, North Carolina, takes notes during a meeting with the elders of the Haqdad Kelay village not far from the Kandahar airport on April 9, 2002. The Psyops missions consist in explaining why more than 5 000 American soldiers are present in Afghanistan, in ascertaining the needs of the populations and helping in the gathering of information.

Below. A Psyops team visits a village south of Kandahar, along with a soldier from the Kabul government serving as interpreter. The men of this unit follow local customs, but have also been trained in psychological warfare and try to bring help to the villagers while at the same time "spreading the good news". *(DOD Pictures)*

made up of eight specialists forming the Special Operations Media System took up turns to broadcast their radio programs, mostly information and music. The team worked in shifts with an American- Afghan element of the 8th Psychological Operations Battalion from Fort Bragg that produces the actual broadcasts.

The programs, as in a normal radio station, consisted of general and non polemical news, good and optimistic information, laced with Afghan songs. The success of this radio also stems from the fact that during their years in power, the Taliban forbade the listening or the

Messages from the sky

After the fall of Kabul and the seizure of Kandahar, one of the AFSOC Commando Solo began to fly on a daily basis directly over Afghanistan in order to broadcast messages and music aimed specifically at the local population. In March, 2002, the Commando Solo flew back to the USA and it was replaced by a Psyops ground element that was located on the Bagram air base, not far from Kabul.

On March 8, the radio became operational and started to broadcast on the same frequencies as the EC-130E (AM and SW) from Bagram and from Kandahar. Depending on weather conditions, short waves broadcasts could cover the whole of Afghanistan, while the AM range was around eighty kilometres. Twenty-four hours a day, the team,

production of any type of music. However, many Afghans still don't know that these broadcasts originated from a radio station belonging to a US Army Psychological Operations unit...

On the whole, the psychological operations conducted by the American Special Forces were a success, something that can be explained by the wide range of modern systems that were used as well as by the vulnerability of a population that had been cut off from any information for years, without mentioning the non-existent Taliban counter-propaganda. The Pentagon, as a matter of fact, played this part very well and with very little time to spare. It did have the advantage of experience on its side though, having practised that sort of unconventional military action on many occasions since the Gulf war and during the years spent policing the Balkans and Africa.

CIVIL AFFAIRS OPERATIONS IN TALIBA

The Civil Affairs units mission is to help the commander of any militar operation to establish connections with civilian authorities and the popula tions they are supposed to control. Their role is to explain the missions American units in the area of operations and to include the local authoriti and populations in the operational plans in order to make sure that the civ lian populations will not suffer unduly from the crisis. Civil Affairs units wo alongside special and conventional forces and they are capable of assistin and helping the remaining civilian administration in the operational zone

Civil Affairs specialists are trained to identify all the primary needs of large civilian population in times of war or during natural disasters. They c also identify the local resources that can help in military operations, cont bute to minimize the civilian implications of military operations, support lo civilian activities when they have a positive impact on friendly forces, pr pare and carry out the evacuations of civilians, participate in anti-narcoti operations, establish and maintain the links between local relief agencies a non governmental agencies as well as with governmental or private co mercial companies.

When accomplishing missions in support of special operations, Civil Affa soldiers are chosen for their knowledge of the operational zone and of t languages of the country they will be operating in. They can also, if neede serve as national defence experts in all sorts of military operations, fro unconventional warfare to high intensity operations. The flexible operati

82

Left.
Spring 2003. Protected by an SF detachment, a CA team from the 450th Civil Affairs Battalion enters an Afghan village. The main tasks of those units is to establish links with local leaders in order to get a better impression of the real needs of the indigeneous population, whether in times of natural disasters or in times of war.
(DOD Picture)

Right.
CA team after its return to the USA at the end of its deployment to Afghanistan. The operational structure of the CA unit makes it capable of replacing a local administration when the latter has disappeared. Today, the 96th Civil Affairs Battalion (Airborne) is the only CA unit in the US Army and it can be deployed at very short notice in support of Special Operation Forces.
(DOD Picture)

OUNTRY

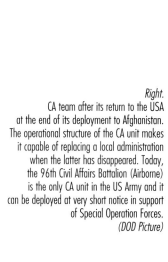

al structure of Civil Affairs units and their vast knowledge make it an asy task for them to substitute themselves for the local administration hen the latter is found wanting or completely absent.

Currently, the 96th Civil Affairs Battalion (Airborne) is the only unit f its kind. Thanks to its parachute training, it can be deployed very viftly in support of special units whenever the need arises.

It is currently made up of 4 % of active duty soldiers, the remaining 6 % belonging to four different Civil Affairs commands of the Army eserve. For specialized units like the CA battalions, the Army Reserve onstitutes a readily available an extraordinary source of trained and xperienced soldiers, in fields as diverse as administration, law and der, public health issues, justice, public finances, education, civil defen-, civil engineering, communication systems, public transportation, food upplies, general economics, cultural affairs, public information and anagement.

In the recent past, Civil Affairs units have taken part in various mili-ry operations: Just Cause in Panama, Desert Shield and Desert Storm the Middle East, the restoration of the Panamanian government during peration Promote Liberty, Restore Hope in Somalia and Enduring Free-m in Afghanistan. Those experts were also used to help in the resto-tion of the Haitian State and in the various operations undertaken in osnia-Herzegovina, in Kosovo and in the Philippines.

Right.
A joint American and British team comprising some CA specialists attends to civilians in a remote Afghan village. CA units have already participated in several military operations in the past: Just Cause in Panama, Desert Shield and Desert Storm in the Middle East, Promote Liberty in Panama to help restauring the Panamean government, Restore Hope in Somalia, Enduring Freedom in Afghanistan (operation still underway) and Iraqi Freedom in Iraq.
(DOD Picture)

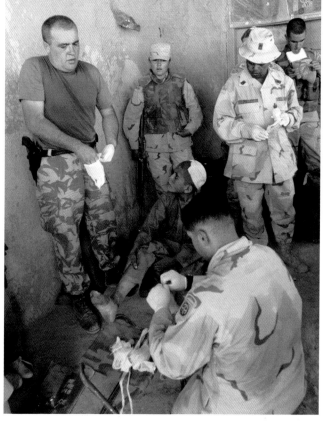

Left.
A team belonging to the Knoxville, Tennessee, based 489th CA battalion performs a water quality test in order to define the salt level of water around the Kandahar airport in May 2002.
(DOD Picture)

The US Air Force, with its special units and its bombardment aircraft, can rightly be considered as one of the major players in the victory of the American forces in Afghanistan. From the end of September 2001, the USAF special units had been inserted around the country.

Before achieving this, the United States had to exert a certain amount of pressure on Pakistan, Uzbekistan and Tajikistan - as regards these last two countries, the USA had to ask the Russian government to help—in order to be able to position their special forces and their aviation and UAV supports.

The US Air Force Special Forces were naturally, with their Army and Navy counterparts, among the first American units to be deployed, mainly in Pakistan and in Uzbekistan.

Discreetly, assuming the identity of 10th Mountain Division troopers — which was to serve as a "cover" for many special units during the conflict-, teams of tactical air controllers landed in Termez during the last week of September 2001. At this forward operation base, the CCTs (Combat Control Teams) discovered the sorry state of the runway and of the control tower "*fitted with equipments dating back to the fifties*". So the Air Force commandos preferred to use their own radio equipment, in particular the MMLS system (experimented for the first time in Bosnia, but never previously in real combat operations). Even in the worst climatic conditions - as is normally the case in Uzbekistan at that time of the year-, this radio set gives its operator the exact position of the runway and insures quality all-weather landings. CCT teams worked twenty-four hours a day to guide in the never-ending stream of aircraft, the first of which was a C-17 Globemaster III which brought in the first elements of the base camp.

With America's best on the borders

At the same time, Special Forces teams of Army SF and Navy SEALs, always reinforced with one or two CCT, were formed. They were ready on the borders to operate in Taliban country. On Sunday, October 7, bombardments began on Afghanistan. (Officially, American and British Special Forces waited twelve days after the start of those bombardments before intervening.)

The SF then took advantage of the airborne operation launched on October 19, 2001, by about a hundred Rangers dropped by MC-130 Combat Talon II of the 15th SOS, one MC-130H / P of the 17th SOS and then extracted by MH-53J Pave Low of the 17th SOS and MH-60G of the 55th SOS. Their mission was officially to seize and control an airstrip in the South of Afghanistan in the vicinity of Kandahar, but their real job was in fact to deceive the enemy forces. More than fifteen Special Forces teams consisting of Special Forces/SEAL/CCT/CWT were then inserted at night by helicopters in the North and the central Eastern part of the country. Their mission: to help the Northern Alliance to win against the much more powerful Taliban forces. These teams were infiltrated by MH-53J Pave Low helicopters belonging to the 20th SOS in the North, and MH-60J belonging to the 55th SOS in the South of Afghanistan. Just a day before, the first teams had penetrated into Taliban country, by helicopters; In the next few days, armament and equipment for the Afghan anti-Taliban groups was airlifted by MC-

A Combat Talon III coming in to land during operation *Enduring Freedom*. Just like the AC-130 "Gunships" proved instrumental in the delivery of around-the-clock air support, the Combat Talon III were irreplaceable when it came to the insertion of SF teams or the tracking of the last remaining Taliban in the South of the country.
(USAF Picture)

130E / H Combat Talon I and II of the 15th SOS (later to be joined by 1st SOS aircraft).

The different teams were then taken into the care of the various factions of the Northern Alliance. After a few days or a few weeks for some, those teams were ready to join in the fray.

For example, CCT Technical Sergeant Calvin...., who first set foot on Afghan soil on October 19, began guiding Coalition attack aircrafts on Taliban positions in front of Bagram airport, in the central Eastern part of the country, near Kabul less than thirty hours after his arrival. For the past three years, the front had been static in this region and the enemies had had time to dig in a series of fortifications. Repeatedly, very well armed Talibans opened fire on the American team, firing at them over open sights. "*We had set up our position on a hill that was overlooking Taliban positions when we finally chose a target, an enemy headquarters. I then asked for my first CAS (Close Air Support) mission, and a Navy aircraft arrived and released its bombs on target*", said the CCT sergeant. "*The building disappeared, totally destroyed. The Afghan fighters around us then understood that we were there to help them.*" CAS missions went on uninterrupted day and night, with all the different types of aircraft currently in the USAF and US Navy inventory. "*We had to ask for hundreds of CAS missions during these twenty-five days, because the valley was literally covered with tanks, armoured cars and bunkers.*"

At the same time, AC-130H / U "Gunships" of the 4th and 16th SOS based in Uzbekistan and in Pakistan began their CAS operations in support of SF teams and anti-Taliban forces. In support of those CAS missions, psychological air operations began on October 17, 2001, with EC-130E Commando Solo broadcasting radio messages aimed at the local population and at the Talibans. Between October 18 and December 7, 2001, almost twenty-four hours a day, the various AFSOC aircrafts roamed the Afghan skies to infiltrate and extract SF teams and their Afghan allies while delivering tons of supplies. Even today, AC-130s continue to support various ground operations, while some Combat Talon II are still based in Afghanistan to airlift supplies to the various Special Forces camps of the Coalition.

The collapse of the Talibans in twenty-five days

As soon as the North of the country fell into the hands of the Northern Alliance, the Kabul front soon collapsed. The operations aiming to seize the capital were expected to last six months; in fact, less than twenty-five days were sufficient to oust the Talibans from the city as they were literally crushed by the American air power. In the end, Sergeant Calvin's group made up of AFSOC airmen was given the honour of freeing the American embassy in Kabul that had been abandoned since 1989.

VICTORY FOR THE USAF SPECIAL FORCE

Air Force Special Operations Command units

● **The 16th Special Operations Group,** located in Hurlburt Field, Florida is the largest and oldest AFSOC unit. Being on call for CENTCOM, SOUTHCOM and other commands, it is also the most overworked AFSOC unit.
— 4th Special Operations Squadron (AC-130U)
— 8th Special Operations Squadron (MC-130E)
— 9th Special Operations Squadron (MC-130N)
— 15th Special Operations Squadron (MC-130H);
— 16th Special Operations Squadron (AC-130H)
— 20th Special Operations Squadron (MH-53J).

● **The193rd Special Operations Wing,** Harrisburg, Middeltown, Pennsylvania,
— 193rd Special Operations Squadron (EC-130E)
— 107th Air Weather Flight
— 123rd Special Tactics Flight
— 146th Air Weather Flight
— 181st Air Weather Flight
— 280th Combat Communications Squadron.

● **The 352nd Special Operations Group,** Mildenhall, United Kingdom, under CENTCOM.
— 7th Special Operations Squadron (MC-130H)
— 21st Special Operations Squadron (MH-53J)
— 67th Special Operations Squadron (MC-130N/P).

● **The 353nd Special Operations Group,** Kadena, Okinawa, Japan, under Pacific Command.
— 1st Special Operations Squadron (MC-130H);
— 17th Special Operations Squadron (MC-130N/P);
— 31st Special Operations Squadron (MH-53J) ;
— 427th Special Operations Squadron (CASA C.212).

● **The 919th Special Operations Wing/919th Operations Group,** Duke Field, Florida, belonging to the Air Reserve.
— 5th Special Operations Squadron (MC-130N/P)
— 17th Special Operations Squadron (MC-130E).

● **The 58th Special Operations Wing/58th Operations Group,** Kirtland, New Mexico.
— 512nd Special Operations Squadron (UH-1N, MH-60G)
— 550th Special Operations Squadron (MC-130N/P, MC-130H, MH-53J).

● **The 720th Special Tactics Group,** Hurlburt Field, Florida, made up of Air Combat Controllers for tactical air control, of Pararescuemen for Combat Search And Rescue and of Combat Weathermen tasked with the gathering of weather-related intelligence for the higher command.
— 21st Special Tactics Squadron
— 22nd Special Tactics Squadron
— 23rd Special Tactics Squadron
— 24st Special Tactics Squadron
— 10th Combat Weather Squadron.

● **The Air Force Special Operations School** in Hurlburt Field, Florida.

● **The 18th Flight Test Squadron,** Hurlburt Field, Florida.

The inventory of the AFSOC

THE AFSOC is equipped with:

— Eight AC-130H Spectre,
— Thirteen AC-130U Spooky,
— Thirty six MH-53J Pave Low ,
— Ten MH-60G Pave Hawk ,
— Eight MC-130E Combat Talon I ,
— Twenty-one MC-130H Combat Talon II,
— Five EC-130 Commando Solo,
— Eight EC-130 flying HQ
— Twenty-four MC130P Combat Shadow,
— Two UH-1N.

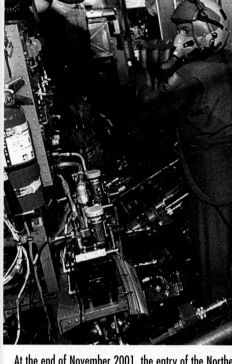

At the end of November 2001, the entry of the Norther Alliance forces into the city of Mazar-e-Sharif represented a important victory for the anti-Taliban, for the American com mand and especially for US Special Forces. Indeed, the seizu re of this city also meant the capture one of the three majo airports in Afghanistan, and the possibility for the American to launch air operations from this base. However, th bomb craters on the runway, the derelict control towe the minefields and the various booby traps left b the Taliban represented a big challenge for th AFSOC commandos. For the Air Combat Contro lers team as well as for a small party of A Force engineers who arrived from Uzbekis tan, the task was simple: to render the airs trip usable in only a few days after havin secured Mazar-e-Sharif. Leading this tea and coming straight out of the Balkh valle Master Sergeant Bart Decker, a face that wo soon to be well known when a picture of hir riding a horse was published in the wester press. "*Our main obstacle was the numbe of booby traps placed around the airpor* explained Bart Decker. "*So we called a mir clearance team which, over several days, ble up tons of bombs, mines and booby trap including a booby-trapped bomb locate under the control tower.*" However, the mai runway was too damaged to be pu straight back into service so the CCTs dec ded to only use one thousand metres o runway that was "*strewn with only eigl craters*". To repair the runway, th Afghans used techniques and materia "*at least hundred years old*", unde the dumbfounded eyes of the Amer cans. And it worked! During a fortnight, planes too off and landed on this bit of runway patched up "*wit chewing gum*".

"*On the other hand, the control tower was in ruins*" said Master Sergeant Decker, "*and even though we ha all the equipment to repair it at once, it would have take us too much time. So, operating from 4X4 vehicles, usin portable lighting equipment and our communication systems, we began to guide in the heavy lift ai*

The US special units in the Afghan sky

The USAF deployed over Afghanistan most of its 16th Special Operations Wing, namely the 4th and 16th Special Operations Squadrons (SOS) equipped with AC-130U and AC-130H "Gunships", the15th SOS equipped with MC-130 Combat Talon II, the 20th SOS equipped with MH-53 Pave Low III, the 55th SOS equipped with MH-60 Pave Hawk; Teams of Combat Controllers and Parescuemen belonging to the 23rd and 24th Special Tactics Squadrons (STS) of the 720th Special Tactics Group and the 320th STS of the 353rd Special Operations Group, as well as some teams belonging to the 10th Combat Weather Squadron of the 720th STG.

Those assets were reinforced by MC-130H Combat Talon II and MH-53J of the 353rd Special Operations Group normally based in Okinawa in Japan and EC-130E Commando Solo from the 193rd Special Operations Wing of the Pennsylvania Air Force National Guard which were sent as an additional reinforcement to the battleground.

raft. "Indeed, the USAF Combat Controllers are the only US SF perators to be qualified to guide in planes on to makeshift airsips, with only a portable radar and a classic radio. Sergeant Decer was given the honour of guiding in the first aircraft to land Mazar-e-Sharif, an AFSOC plane of course!

"Full steam ahead!"

After the fall of Kabul, on November 13, 2001, USSOCOM eams deployed in the North of the country were put on hold, aiting for the new operation zones to be redefined. The eastern zones kept up a relentless operating pace because aliban units were still present in the Kandahar and Garez regions until the middle of December. The special perations command decided not to change the composition of the various Special Forces, SEAL, Rangers, British SAS and SBS and Australian and New Zealand SAS eams who had been until then regularly reinforced with ne or two CCT operators. After the inconclusive Tora Bora peration near Jalalabad in the east of the country at the eginning of December, 2001, the American command decied, from the first week of January, 2002, to launch a series

Top, from left to right.
Close-up on USAF Staff Sergeant Scott Rodatz from the 4th Special Operations Squadron loading a 105 mm round in the breech of the AC-130U "Gunship" howitzer. The USAFSOC "Gunship" fleet will receive a complete mid-life upgrade in 2010, receiving new engines, propeller blades, armour plates, weapon suites, sensors and ammunition.
(USAF Picture)

The Special Tactics Squadrons

The Air Force Special Tactics Squadrons (STS) are composed of several different types of units, including the Combat Controllers Teams (CCT), the Pararescuemen Teams (PT) and the Combat Weather Teams (CWT). In order to create more diversified units for operations, groups are formed with different specializations. Their goal is to establish "bridges" between the parajumpers and ground forces. Thus the Combat Controllers prepare the jumping zone, guide air traffic, designate aviation targets, while the Combat Weather Teams broadcast continuous weather information. The Pararescuemen pick up and treat the wounded. STS elements may also be integrated into a Special Forces Group (as was the case in Afghanistan) for a specific mission. Thus the CCTs worked with the SEAL teams in Panama and others with the Special Forces in Iraq, in Afghanistan, and then again in Iraq.

Reconstruction of an AFSOC sniper.
In order to protect its LZs (Landing Zones), the AFSOC deploys its own sniper trained operators. Armed with SR-16s or SR-25s, they can provide all-round security up to 400 metres when landing in hostile areas. This sniper is equipped with an SR-16 fitted with a RIS on which different accessories like the AN/PAQ-4 or AN/PEQ-2 Laser pointers or, as illustrated here, a Streamlight VL1 torch can be fitted. The uniform is the classic three colours desert BDU over which a TAC-V1 assault vest is worn, completed by a "boonie hat", Nomex aviator gloves and a single knee pad used when firing from the kneeling position.

The Air Force Special Operations Command

The AFSOC is made up of 10 000 regular and reserve officers, NCOs and Airmen, about 22% of whom being deployed outside the USA at any given time.

The AFSOC HQ is located in Hurlburt Field, Fla with most of the AFSOC Wings.

A Special Operations Group (SOG) is based in the United Kingdom and another one in Japan.

To this inventory must also be added two Air Force Reserve Special Operations Wings (SOW) as well as an Air National Guard Squadron.

The AFSOC units are trained to undertake high-intensity warfare operations, unconventional operations, special reconnaissance, friendly states support and counter-terrorism.

The three active-duty units can deploy more than one hundred special operations modified fixed-wings and rotary-wings aircrafts.

Those modified aircrafts are:

The AC-130H Spectre and AC-130U. The missions of those aircrafts include all-weather, around-the-clock close air support including troop in contact support, convoy escort, support of troops involved in operations in urban areas, battlefield air interdiction and protection operation in support of surrounded camps or fire bases.

The EC-130E Commando Solo. The missions of those aircrafts include the conduct of psychological operations from an airborne platform. These operations include radio and TV broadcasts, generally from a high altitude in order to cover the widest possible area.

If necessary, this aircraft can also be used for electronic intelligence gathering (ELINT) or electronic warfare (EW) missions.

The MH-53J/M Pave Low helicopter. The missions of those aircrafts include all-weather day and night long-distance and very low altitude undetected penetration missions of hostile areas in order to insert, extract and replenish special forces units.

The MH-60G Pave Hawk helicopter. Like its "big brother" the MH-53 and even though its avionics are less advanced, the missions of the Pave Hawk include all-weather day and night long-distance and very low altitude undetected penetration missions of hostile areas in order to insert, extract and replenish special forces units.

The MH-60G can also be used for Combat Search And Rescue with the appropriate crew.

The MC-130E Combat Talon I and **MC-130H Combat Talon II**. The missions of those aircrafts include all-weather, around-the-clock insertion, extraction and replenishment of American and Allied special units.

The MC-130P Combat Shadow. The missions of those aircrafts include all-weather, around-the-clock insertion, extraction and replenishment of American and Allied special units as well as the air-refuelling of other AFSOC aircrafts.

Above.
The AFSOC fleet of Pave Low helicopters was used intensively during the Afghan operations, more than 80% of the total number of those aircrafts being at some point in the conflict present in or around Afghanistan. Another MH-53J/M pair was also deployed at the same time in the Philippines in support of operations against the local Muslim guerrilla.
(USAF Picture)

zone by zone search operations along the border with akistan. This huge undertaking was supported from the air USAFSOC AC-130 "Gunships" operating in support of ground oops. The air to ground liaison between the ground elements nd the Air Force was of course devoted to the CCTs. Staff Ser-ant Eric.... of the 23rd Special Tactics Squadron who was erating with some SEALs takes up the story: "*Our team's mis-on was to search a zone riddled with about fifty caves, tun-els and surface structures, in order to check whether anybo-was hiding there. Initially, the mission was supposed to last r ten hours but it ended up lasting for nine days! Although ur allocated area had previously been "softened up" by the r Force, everything was considered as hostile. So while the ALs searched the tunnels, we were waiting outside, ready to ll in air support. The Air Force was constantly roaming, rea-to deliver deadly close air support and reporting any move-ents of troops or vehicles in the area.*" If the team of Ser-ant Eric did not find any "Al-Qaida's" members, on the other nd, they discovered an important stock of weapons and docu-ents. "*In one of the tunnels, we discovered mountains of mmunition, communication equipments, fuel tanks, a sub-rranean hospital and even toilets complete with toilet paper!* fter all the interesting documents had been recovered, the ALs demolition specialists blew up the tunnels. The CCTs then lled in air support to complete the destruction. " *However, uring this operation, we went back a day later on to one of e tunnels we had blown up earlier and realized it had not en completely destroyed.* "In fact, we discovered that nume-us tunnels were reinforced with concrete and steel, so that ey were very sturdy. The teams were then looking for a way destroying these tunnels once and for all. "*One of the obs-cles was that we had no accurate maps. When you commu-cate with a pilot to indicate a target, it is necessary to unders-nd that, from his point of view, mountains and deserts appear identical and that there is not a huge difference between a ries of cliffs and another one.* "So, with nothing more than GPS, a pencil and a note pad, the CCTs established "maps" of e tunnels." *To give accurate grid coordinates as well as the*

Right.
Last minute check-list for a 352nd Special Operations Group MC-130P crewmember. The various AFSOC units (active-duty, National Guard and Reserve) all rotate through the Afghan theatre of operations.
(USAF Picture)

The successes of the "Gunships"

Following a number of after action reports concerning the successes of AC-130 during air operations over Afghanistan, the US Air Forces has decided, in March 2002, to modify another four C-130H Hercules transport aircraft into the "Gunship" AC-130U Spectre configuration.

These aircrafts should be operational by the summer of 2003. Quickly deployed to airstrips in Uzbekistan and in Pakistan, various AC-130U and AC-130H provided, on a daily basis and almost twenty-four hours a day, close air support for special and conventional troops in contact.

Some said that the "Gunships" had often had to take on the role of the rather absent and criticized American artillery to support ground units engaged in the different operations. Fortunately, the American and later the French air forces were omnipresent, bringing in round-the-clock support, without ever meeting any serious antiaircraft threat.

Left.
Last check before take off for a "flight" of AC-130U Spooky belonging to the 4th SOS of the 16th Special Operations Wing. *(USAF Picture)*

Right.
An Hurlburt Field Fla based 4th Special Operations Squadron AC-130U crewmember. *(USAF Picture)*

During the Afghan conflict, the 16th Special Operations Wing rotated all of its "Gunships", (AC-130H and AC-130U) in theatre with the mission of crushing the enemy under a hail of lead and fire whenever TICs (Troops In Contact) requested air support. (USAF Picture)

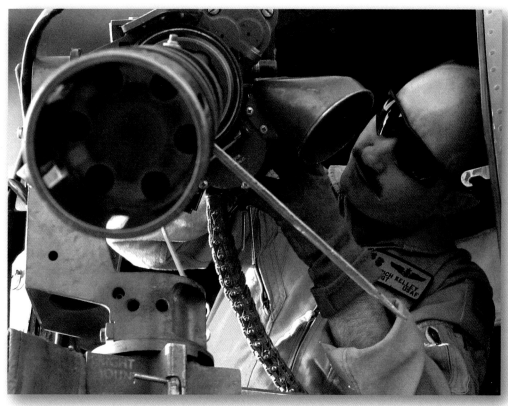

...yout of a tunnel" continued the 23rd STS sergeant, "we had ...draw a sketch of each tunnel. And every time it took hours ...measure the inside and the outside of the site, and to put ...gether a decent target report for the pilots."

Several CCTs participated in the famous battle of Takur Ghar ...ee page 62); one of them, Technical Sergeant John A. Chapman ...as killed on March 4, 2002, during the rescue operation of a ...avy SEAL, Petty Officer Neil Roberts, who had, a few hours befo-..., fallen from a Chinook helicopter. During this action, the role ...the CCTs was instrumental, calling in close air support only a few ...eters in front of the American positions, thus saving the soldiers ...ho had escaped the helicopter crash. "*I was in the base camp, ...iles away from any action,*" remembers Staff Sergeant Gabe ...own, Air Combat Controller of the 22nd Special Tactics Squa-...on, "*when I heard that a helicopter had been shot down. Put-...ng on my combat rig straight away, I jumped into the rescue chopper. We had not yet landed when our chopper had already taken several roc-kets and small arms hits. There was blood everywhere and within seconds four of us had been killed. Without thin-king, we jumped of this hell, while Rangers fired like mad at the bad guys.*" The CCT sergeant ran for the shelter of a rock and started to unpack his kit, knowing that only close air support will be able to save them consi-dering the dispro-portion of forces, the enemy being at least ten times as numerous as they were. "*Shots rang out everywhere, and it is almost surrealistic to think that, busying* myself with the job at hand, I did not think at all about the dan-ger." But reality came back to him very quickly when Gabe Brown saw a group of Moslem fundamentalists charging towards them out of their bunkers at his 9 o'clock." I *had an attack aircraft armed with 250 kilos bombs over us, but "the bad guys" were too close to our position. So, I told him to do a gun pass with his onboard cannon. That's exactly what he did, at a very, very low altitude. I could see snow flying everywhere around the bunker of those bas-tards and I knew the shells were hitting home!*" The aircraft did several gun runs until he ran out of ammo and then it disappea-red with a deafening roar.

"*Good God!*" thought Brown, in spite of several thousand rounds expanded on their positions, the " Al-Qaida " gunmen continued to fire. We had now been sitting here for over two hours and the situa-tion was worsening. Any movement was impossible. "*Request some frags* (fragmentation bombs)"! yelled the platoon leader looking at me straight in the eyes. At this range, we stood every chance of being killed by our own tac air, but it was the only solution because "the bad guys" began to surround us and the aviation had warned us that enemy reinforcements arrived. "

The attack aircrafts started their bombing runs on the Taliban positions. "*The noise level was such that it reminded me of war films, and I could smell burning pine trees and earth turned to dirty snow.*" Given the distance, the CCT sergeant did not use his Tactical Laser Designator; he simply gave the planes a simple mark like a small tree that he would nickname the "bonsaï". When the smoke clea-red, the only reminder of the "bonsaï" was a smoking stick. Enemy resistance was finally broken and, for the first time in fourteen hours, Gabe Brown could hiss a breath of relief. Around him were strewn the bodies of seven American soldiers, including a Pararescueman, Senior Airman Jason Cunningham. In the dark of night, the survi-ving commandos were extracted by helicopter from the area.

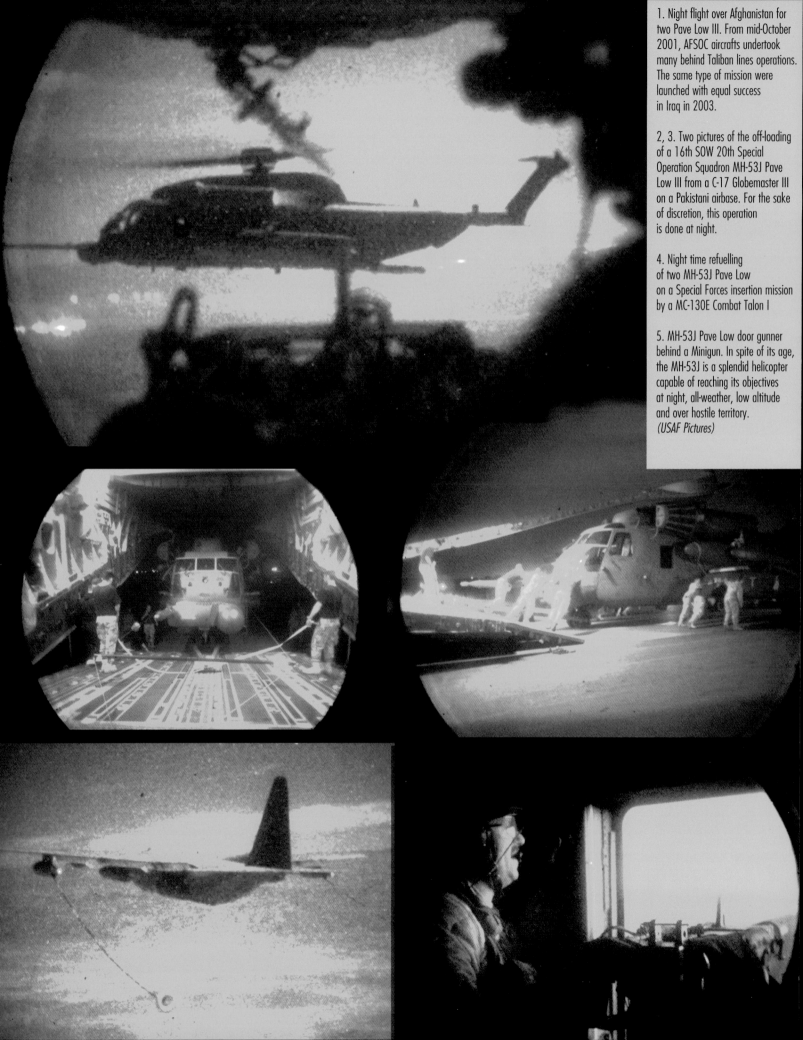

1. Night flight over Afghanistan for two Pave Low III. From mid-October 2001, AFSOC aircrafts undertook many behind Taliban lines operations. The same type of mission were launched with equal success in Iraq in 2003.

2, 3. Two pictures of the off-loading of a 16th SOW 20th Special Operation Squadron MH-53J Pave Low III from a C-17 Globemaster III on a Pakistani airbase. For the sake of discretion, this operation is done at night.

4. Night time refuelling of two MH-53J Pave Low on a Special Forces insertion mission by a MC-130E Combat Talon I

5. MH-53J Pave Low door gunner behind a Minigun. In spite of its age, the MH-53J is a splendid helicopter capable of reaching its objectives at night, all-weather, low altitude and over hostile territory.
(USAF Pictures)

The CCT, PJ AND CWS on operation

The 720th Special Tactics Group (STG) was created in 1987, at Hurlburt Field, Florida. This unit is made up of Air Combat Controllers Teams, Pararescuemen Teams (400 men strong) in charge of combat search and rescue operations and, since 1996, of a Combat Weather Squadron (CWS) which is a combat meteorological unit, in charge of providing accurate forecasts in a combat environment and made up of a total of five detachments (120 men altogether). Those units represent a total of 800 operational commandos organized around the 21st, 22nd, 23rd, 24th and 10th Weather Squadrons, as well as the 320th and 321st, based respectively in Japan and in Great Britain.

During Enduring Freedom, hundreds of CCTs, Pararescuemen and Weathermen operated in Afghanistan, including eleven commandos belonging to the 23rd STS who accounted for no less than 175 close air support missions on the frontline in twenty five days.

The operations continue

During *operation Anaconda* in March, 2002, AC-130s were, of course, always present in the sky, often providing close air support to ground units in difficult positions. The very same thing happened in May during *Operation Condor* that was, by all reckoning, less intense than the previous ones and finally during *Operation Buzzard*, at the end of May. Meanwhile, at the end of January, the first contingent of AFSOC personnel returned to the USA, immediately replaced by another reduced one, because the threat was perceived as being less important than previously. On April 15, 2002, sergeant Dave..... of the 20th Special Operations Squadron received the Purple Heart for wounds received during operation Enduring Freedom. He was wounded at the conclusion of a rescue mission, in November, 2001, when his helicopter came under Taliban fire.

But on June 12 at 1300, an MC-130H Combat Talon II crashed near the Band-e-Sardeh dam, eighty kilometres southeast of Gardez, in the Paktiha province and caught fire. Two AFSOC commandos and a green beret were killed, and seven other were wounded (five AFSOC members and two Army soldiers). This aircraft had been supposed to resupply a Special Forces patrol operating in the area and then to bring three SF operators back to Kandahar.

Above.
the sun rises for this 16th SOS MC-130E loadmaster as his aircraft flies back to Bagram after a ressuply mission on an advanced air base in the South of Afghanistan.
(USAF Picture)

AFSOC CCT in Afghanistan during the winter of 2001.
This CCT depicts one of the Combat Controllers that were inserted into Afghanistan amidst other Coalition special units (SF, SEAL, SAS, SBS) in order to coordinate and guide tactical air support and reopen abandoned and derelict airfields. This 23rd STS operator uses his PVS-18 to locate possible sentries on an operation with US Navy SEALs. He is armed with a LAM (Laser Aiming Module) equipped HK SOCOM Mark 23 .45ACP suppressed pistol which is well suited to this task. The three colours desert BDU has been altered by the adding of sleeve pockets and Velcro-mounted patches and rank insignias and over his body armour, this NCO wears a Blackhawk Omega assault vest. A Wilcox Mark 23-specific holster is also secured to his right thigh.

THE USAF COMBAT CONTROL TEAMS IN

Certainly the least well-known of the American Special Forces before the Afghan war, the Combat Controllers, Pararescuemen and Combat Weathermen of the 720th Special Tactics Group played a starring role during these hostilities, where they were present from Day 1.

Recently created, in October 1987, the unit is made up of 800 soldiers in seven squadrons (Special Tactics Squadrons), located in the USA, Europe and Southeast Asia.

The mission of the CCTs is to guide the planes during bombings and providing fire cover, and to do air traffic control at an airport or even on a makeshift airstrip.

Thus the CCTs may work with airborne troops who have taken an airfield in enemy territory and guide the assault-troop landing planes or planes with fresh troops and equipment. In Somalia, for example, during *Operation United Shield*, teams from the 23rd Special Tactics Squadron directed air traffic for 72 hours at the Mogadiscio airport and guided more than 150 planes. (Note that the CCTs are not the same as the Tactical Air Control Parties, whose soldiers are not part of the 720th STG.)

"EYES ON THE TARGET"

The CCTs are especially the first to intervene in enemy territory. Their motto is "*First here*". Thus during a helicopter or parachute operation the CTs jump first with their transmission

Opposite, left.
...very well known picture of a CCT providing close security for a USAID ...nvoy to Khwaja Bahuaddin on November the 15th 2001, a mission ...r removed from tactical air control but made nevertheless possible ...anks to the very thorough training each CCT receives during his years ...f formation. This operator carries a Harris Falcon II tactical radio ...his rucksack. *(Brennan Linsley/AP/SIPA Press Picture)*

Opposite, right.
A USAF Combat Controller belonging to a Special Tactics Squadron during a training exercise undertaken during Operation Enduring Freedom. The "home-made" contraption on his helmet is noteworthy.
(USAF Picture)

...ottom, left.
...r Force Reserve Combat Controller Technical Sergeant Jim Hotaling ...oviding security to a Special Forces team in a village ...the South of Afghanistan during the 2001-2002 winter. A total ...about one hundred CCTs, Pararescuemen and Combat Weathermen ...perated in Afghanistan and in Pakistan during the campaign.
...OD Picture)

Bottom right.
...his picture of Air Force Combat Controller Master Sergeant Bart Decker ...riding a horse among Northern Alliance troops was the first picture ...eleased by the Pentagon of special units on operations in Afghanistan. Master Sergeant Bart Decker was latter to be given the honour of guiding in the first American aircraft which landed i n Mazar-e-Sharif after that city fell.
(USAF Picture)

CCT TRAINING

USAFSOC has recently started a new training syllabus for its special operators in its Combat Control School of Pope Air Force Base in North Carolina. Before being allowed to wear the scarlet beret which is their trademark, the aspiring CCTs have to undergo a twelve to fifteen-month long course which addresses airmen, NCOs and officers alike.

Four courses are run yearly with an average of eleven students per course. As an example, course 02-01 graduated ten operators out of thirteen hopefuls who came from varied backgrounds including ex-Rangers, SEALs and Marine Recons.

The actual training takes place in Pope AFB (14 weeks) and in six other locations. Small units tactics, land navigation and communications are taught in Lackland, Texas, during 10 weeks; SCUBA diving is taught at the Key West Florida Army Diving School during 4 weeks; the static-line parachute course takes place at the Army Airborne School in Fort Benning, Georgia during 3 weeks; the survival course at the USAF Survival School in Fairchild, Washington during two-and-a-half weeks; the ditched aircraft escape course on the Navy Pensacola Florida Base during one day; the HALO free-fall parachuting course in Fort Bragg, North Carolina and Yuma, Arizona during 5 weeks; and the air traffic, air communication and radar procedures course in Kessler AFB, Missouri during another 15 weeks-and-a-half.

...nd target-designating equipment. The first CCT wartime jump ...ook place during *Operation Just Cause* in Panama with the ...rd Rangers batallion, amidst the tracer bullets fired by the ...anamanians.

In Afghanistan, the eleven Combat Controllers (knicknamed ...he "eyes on the target"), integrated into the Special Forces ...eams participating in the fighting, guided 175 bombing mis-

sions (by F-16 or B-52 fighter-bombers), non-stop during 25 days.

Less than a year later the Combat Controllers were back at it again, this time in Iraq, both in the south of the country with autonomous Special Forces teams sent in before the main troops, and in the north with the Kurds to guide the bombings.

Quite an achievement for this newy-created unit !

...HE THICK OF IT

CCT TRAINING

Top. Two CCT students field-stripping their M-4s during their fifteen-month long training course on one of the Pope AFB training areas. CCT Teams are located on six different bases around the world. *(USAF Picture)*

Opposite and bottom.
Different pictures showing various phases of CCT training in the different US Armed Forces schools. When the aspiring CCTs whom, for the best part originate from other special units have undertaken all their training courses, most of them are HALO/HAHO, SCUBA and air traffic control qualified. *(USAF Picture)*

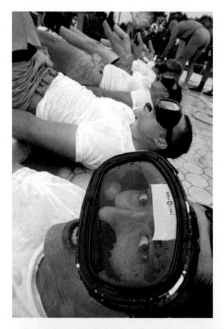

Opposite, right:
precision shooting training for that CCT student before his admittance into the 720th Special Tactics Groups. *(USAF Picture)*

Bottom, left to right. The ancestors of the CCTs are the WW2-era Pathfinders but their main claim to glory lays in the Vietnam-era when teams worked alongside Laotian General Vang Pao as Forward Air Controllers (FACs) against North-Vietnamese infiltrators in Laos. From the beginning of the eighties, CCTs were associated to Pararescuemen in combined units called Special Tactics Squadrons. After their achievements in Afghanistan and Iraq, the CCTs are now also training several foreign teams in their techniques. *(USAF Picture)*

USAFSOC 23rd STS Staff Sergeant "Mike" (name withheld for security reasons) receiving the Purple Heart from the hands of USAFSOC Commander General Maxwell C. Bailey on the 26th of November 2001 for his action during operations around Mazar-e-Sharif during which he had been wounded with five other Special Forces operators. *(USAF Picture)*

97

In Ramstein, Germany, on September 27, 2001, the first Air Force RESCO team awaited the order to take off for Uzbekistan on board a giant C-5. But the Uzbek government had not yet given the green light, fearing border incidents if U.S. soldiers arrived on their soil. On the other hand, as far as "RESCO cover" of southern Afghanistan was concerned, a RESCO team took off from Oman and soon set up quarters in Pakistan on one of the desert air bases there.

On October 1, 2001, General Myers, Army Chief of Staff, on a quick tour in central Asia, was able to meet with Uzbek officials. He declared that it would take about ten days before a RESCO unit could be perfectly operational over the northern zone of Afghanistan. This was because the air base chosen in Uzbekistan could only accept five flights a day, was closed at night, and was too small for C-5s. It finally took sixty-seven round trips in C-17s to bring in all the personnel, helicopters and equipment.

Day and night

The 71st Rescue Squadron (officially the 71st Expeditionary Rescue Squadron or ERSQ) was deployed starting in November 2001 to be operational on December 5. The 71st got in a total of 5500 hours over Afghanistan. The Squadron undertook a multitude of very-low-altitude flights in moutainous regions, day and night, search missions involving downed planes, as well as aircraft and motor vehicle rescue, and even rescue at sea of ships in difficulty in the Indian Ocean. For example the 71st participated in rescue operations resulting from a KC-130 accident, and a downed Pakistani Mirage. It dropped Pararescuemen in the combat zone to treat and evacuate a wounded Australian SAS, also Canadian soldiers hit by friendly fire near Kandahar, and participated in a rescue mission involving the crew of a MC-130H Talon II.

The unit had at its disposal an HC-130, allowing in-flight refueling for rescue helicopters, dropping of Pararescuemen, and transportation of equipment to be dropped over advance positions.

The 71st ERSQ 1 was joined by the 41st RRSQ at the Kandahar airport in southern Afghanistan. This unit was composed of 12 men and two HH-60 Pave Hawk helicopters arriving from Manas in Kirghistan where it had been involved in aircraft rescue operations, and heading for bombing and support missions over Afghanistan.

Above right. An HH-60 Pave Hawk from one of the RESCO units deployed over Afghanistan, during search operations in the southeastern part of the country. From December 5, 2001, the 71st Expeditionary Rescue Squadron was operational in Uzbekistan and "covered" all the northern part of Afghanistan. *(USAF Picture)*

Opposite. During a hostage recovery exercise, view of the portside machine gunner's seat on an HH-60 Pave Hawk. Note the evacuation system for the rapid-fire rotary-barrel GAU-2 ammunition, insuring hefty fire power during RESCO operations (USAF). *(USAF Picture)*

Far right. In May 2002, on a routine mission during Enduring Freedom, under the watchful eye of the tank master, two HH-60 Pave Hawks from the 305th Rescue Squadron are being refueled by an HC-130 from the 332nd Expeditionary Rescue Squadron. These two Reserve units worked together not only over Afghanistan but also in Iraq during Operation Southern Watch. *(USAF Picture)*

---

1. The unit was replaced by the 38th Rescue Squadron.

RESCO OVER AFGHANIS

Opposite left.
An HC-130 tank master from the 39th Rescue Squadron, Master Sergeant Donnie, guides the flight of the HH-60 under the back side of the aircraft toward one of the refueling rods situated under its wings.
(USAF Picture)

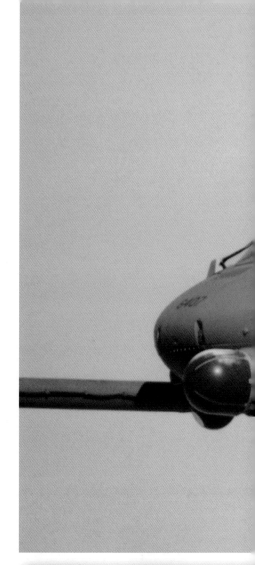

Opposite right.
An HH-60 Pave Hawk from the 66th Rescue Squadron participating in a RESCO exercise. The RESCO units deployed during *Operation Enduring Freedom* chalked up an enormous number of flying hours and saved several dozen coalition soldiers, often under enemy fire and in difficult weather conditions. *(USAF Picture)*

Below left.
A close-up of one of the 33rd RSQ HH-60G Pave Hawk pilots belonging to the 347th Rescue Wing stationed at Moody Air Force Base in the USA. Notice his unit badge, known as "Jolly Green", inspired by the MH-53 Jolly Green Giant squads of the Vietnam War.
(USAF Picture)

Below right, from top to bottom.
The helicopters flew in tough mechanical conditions, and numerous hours were required for machine checks and repairs. Here Senior Airman Patrick Way of the 41st Maintenance Squadron checks the rotor of an HH-60G Pave Hawk during the summer of 2002, before a RESCO training mission in Afghanistan.
(USAF Picture)

In August 2002, before an Afghanistan operation, Staff Sergeant Richie Kelley of the 66th Rescue Squadron rechecks the cable used for hoisting the wounded.
(USAF Picture)

Following page, lower right and from top to bottom.
An HH-60 Pave Hawk team checks out its equipment in preparation for a night exercise in the desert. After flying thousands of hours in Afghanistan, the Air Force RESCO units carried out a dozen or so rescue missions involving American personnel in Iraq. These included one right in the suburbs of Bagdad, an impossible assignment unless the pilot is a real pro!
(USAF Picture)

Night refueling of a Rescue Squadron HH-60 observed through a JVN from another Pave Hawk. Even though their missions were very numerous and very risky, Rescue Squadron losses in Afghanistan were minimal. They lost "only" one Pave Hawk in March 2003.
(USAF Picture)

Under enemy fire

During the night of March 2, 2002, as part of Operation Anaconda, two H-60 Pave Hawks from the 66th Expeditionary Rescue Squadron took off to evacuate wounded soldiers in a valley surrounded on three sides by Taliban forces. The first machine, Gecko 11, entered the valley very low through a curtain of enemy fire coming from small-caliber guns. As soon as her wheels touched down the Pave Hawk became the target of machine guns, mortars and RPG-7 rocket launchers. A mortar shell exploded less than 10 meters away. And while the Pararescuemen were transporting one of the wounded to the helicopter, the crew guided the second chopper, as an AC-130 high above provided cover and pounded the enemy positions.

During that night Gecko 11 and Gecko 12 saved nine wounded soldiers. The next day the two crews had to undertake the same type of rescue operation, but this time they had advance warning that the enemy was still holding its positions. After a flight of only several minutes, the mission was cancelled. But the reprieve was short, for fourteen hours later the two Pave Hawks again swept down the valley, Gecko 11 landing first, then Gecko 12, in the middle of a mortar attack. After picking up the wounded, the helicopters landed in a refueling zone with only nine minutes of fuel left in the tanks.

Three more lives were saved that night. The seventeen heroes who took part in these two operations were awarded the Distinguished Flying Cross in November, 2002.

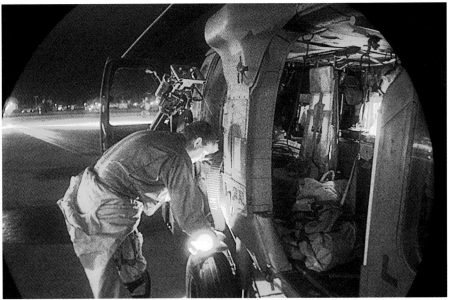

Overloaded among the moutain peaks

On April 3, 2003, two Air Force helicopter pilots were awarded the Most Deserving Pilot prize. One, Major Leighton Anderson, was an MH-53M Pave Low III pilot. The other, Major Edward Lengel, was a RESCO pilot on an MH-60 Pave Hawk who had undertaken a thrilling mission during *Operation Anaconda* in March 2002 to save wounded soldiers.

On the ground, while he was waiting for his Pararescuemen to come back on board, and the enemy was shooting away at his helicopter, Lengel directed the fire from an AC-130 Gunship onto the enemy positions.

Above. A 66th Rescue Squadron HH-60 Pave Hawk during in-flight refueling with an MC-130E Combat Talon from the 711th Special Operations Wing. During *Operation Enduring Freedom*, the RESCO units often worked with Air Force Special Operations units, usually in difficult geographical and weather conditions. *(USAF Picture)*

Opposite. A Pararescueman, crew member of one of the HH-60 helicopters belonging to the 66th Rescue Squadron, checks the radio communications systems before a mission. More than a week before the beginning of air operations over Afghanistan, RESCO units were already in place around the country, in totally forbidden zones. *(USAF Picture)*

Below left. August 15, 2002. The crew of an HH-60G Pave Hawk from the 41st Rescue Squadron, a few minutes before a mission, at the break of dawn, on an advance airstrip somewhere in southern Afghanistan. *(USAF Picture)*

Opposite page. From one of the side doors, Staff Sergeant Tara Miller, tank master of the 71st Expeditionary Rescue Squadron, guides an HH-60 Pave Hawk during a refueling maneuver with an HC-130P King in July 2002 over Afghanistan. *(USAF Picture)*

In that way the four Pararescuemen were able to get four wounded soldiers into the chopper. But the helicopter was overloaded and had to fly over enemy positions in the high mountains. It was then that Lengel piloted his helicopter at low level along a stream for what seemed to be an eternity, until he could finally muster up enough speed to take off.

During the first year of operations, the Air Force RESCO units had not a single accident. However on March 23, 2003, an HH-60 Pave Hawk crashed in southern Afghanistan, killing the six crew members (from the 38th and 41st Rescue Squadrons).

The RESCO

The US Air Force CSAR resources are placed under the control of the Air Combat Command (ACC) and the Air Force Special Operations Command (AFSOC). In all, the Air Force has about one hundred HH-60G Pave Hawks completely equiped for CSAR missions, plus the MH-60s of the Special Forces, which specialize in clandestine Special Forces insertion and extraction. However the MH-60s can also be used for Combat SAR. These machines are all equiped with the latest materials and techniques developed for Combat SAR during the last thirty-five years, of which one of the most important is in-flight refueling.

Starting in 2001, the CIA's boss, George J. Tenet, managed to recruit some two hundred new covert operators for the Agency's Special Operation Group; this was a ten-fold increase over the recruitments undertaken by his predecessor in the eighties. However, in September 2001, only half of those operators were considered operational and most were still training at The Farm, the CIA's training centre in the State of Virginia. The training syllabus was then shortened by a few months (it normally lasts one year) in order to deploy more operators on the ground as soon as possible.

The CIA knows Afghanistan very well. In 1999, the agency had started training about fifty Pakistani secret services independent from the ISI (the intelligence of the Pakistani army) whose mission, if it had not been cancelled by general Mucharaf's coup, was to infiltrate in Afghanistan and to arrest Ben Laden. But Langley also had another ace in its sleeve in the form of a ten-man team of Afghan CIA agents who had been trained at great expenses to hunt down Bin Laden in the Gulf States. However, by September 2001, this team even though it was in constant contact with Washington, never had managed to locate Bin Laden or to give accurate information on his whereabouts and safe houses.

A secret program of the CIA was then set up to channel tens of million of dollars to Afghanistan to help and arm the Northern Alliance. After September 4, 2001, this fund went up to 150 millions dollars. However, the designers of this plan had no illusions on the quality of such an alliance, knowing fully well it could turn coat and betray the Americans if the circumstances were no longer in their favour.

As for the Russian and Iranian secret services, they had also been on the ground for much longer than the Americans, assisting the Alliance and exercising a considerable influence on some of the Tajik, Uzbek and Azaras war leaders.

In addition to the provision of advisors, money and equipment to the Northern Alliance, the CIA also sent several covert teams to link up with the Pachtouns leaders in the South of the country who have always opposed the Taliban. From 1998 on, operating from Pakistan, those teams had covertly, or posing as relief workers from humanitarian organizations, entered Afghanistan. By 2000, about ten leaders, belonging mostly to the Pachtoune and Azara ethnic groups, were handpicked by the CIA team operating from Pakistan in order to work for the Americans it times of need.

According to all of the CIA's calculations, winning the war against the Taliban was going to be no picnic. The Agency reckoned that the Taliban forces were twice as numerous as the Northern Alliance, i.e about twenty one thousand against more than forty thousand (including the foreign volunteers).

After September 11, the White House urgently (less than 48 hours after the attack actually) requested the Pentagon for operational plans to attack Afghanistan. The Armed Forces were hard pressed offering such a quick answer, so CENTCOM, the US command responsible for the Middle East and Central Asia declared that it would need months to ferry enough troops to the theatre and then start an attack on the Taliban. That answer was not good enough for Donald Rumsfeld who was thinking in terms of days, not months. He then addressed the CIA boss, George Tenet, who already had all his operators working on how to locate the terrorists and on how to react to those attacks. The Agency then asked all its operational agents, and in particular those of the Division of Operations, to start a no hold-barred program of secret action! After a short period spend analysing the various reports stemming from all the agents on the ground, Tenet reached the conclusion that the best way to operate in Afghanistan would be to regroup most of the SOG operators, reinforce them with a HUMINT and ELINT capability and to have them perform a "classic" covert campaign supported by USSOCOM and air support. On September 13, the CIA boss presented his plan to president George Bush; George Tenet was confident that SOG teams could be provided to each of the most important commanders of the Northern Alliance, whereas teams of USAF CCTs and US Army Special Forces could locate and designate targets for the American strike aircrafts. In the eye of the CIA's boss, the ever-present air support would more than compensate the inferiority of the Northern

Alliance as well as the small number of special operators on the ground.

"How long will it take for the teams to be on the ground?" asked the President of the United States. "A few weeks" was the CIA's boss of counter-terrorist activities answer. In the Pentagon where these news quickly spread out, nobody considered such an undertaking possible in such a short period of time.

If the CIA boss was so confident in his ability to be on time, it is because he knew he had several aces up his sleeves. Having several operators already in the region, he received up-to-date information on the situation. The quality of those information was soon reinforced by the very discreet fielding in Uzbekistan of a series of Predator drones that could relay in almost real time information coming from Afghanistan and even, if necessary, fire Hellfire missiles on terrorists targets deep inside Afghanistan. That capability of the Predator was kept secret by George Tenet in order to save it for a crucial target when the time would be right.

In front of this barely concealed CIA attack against its interests, the Pentagon decided to react, and within twenty-four hours, the military presented a plan to the White House. This attack plan combined cruise missiles, Air Force bombers and Army and Air Force special operation units "to paint" the targets on the ground with laser markers. However, the Pentagon planning team asked for a minimum of ten days before its special units could actually be ready to operate on the ground in Afghanistan.

The perceived advantage behind the dispatch of only a handful of special forces soldiers to Afghanistan was to give the rest of the world the impression that the USA were not trying to invade another country but were simply involved in the forceful removal of a dangerous regime.

The fear of the USA was to get bogged down in Afghanistan like the British had during the XIXth century or the Soviets during the XXth century.

On September 17, 2001 in the White House, the President signed an order authorizing the CIA to operate "with authorizations" in Afghanistan with its Special Operation Group, its aviation and its armed drones. President Bush also gave his agreement to all the various measures proposed by the CIA boss which were all aiming at dismantling the "Al-Qaida" networks around the world and at elaborating a range of covert operations in which the hands of the USA were not to appear. The very next day, the various stations of the Agency in Central Asia were buzzing with activity and no less than the CIA's chief of secret operations and his assistant flew to Moscow to ask for the assistance of their Russian counterparts; the American agents were interested in anything pertaining to the Taliban, their "Al-Qaida" allies, their various training camps, s well as intelligence on the Russian's allies of the Northern Alliance that Moscow had been supporting for over ten years.

Four days later, on Friday, September 21, the first SOG team of the Agency was in Uzbekistan with all its equipment (transported by one of the CIA's "airline") in transit from Tajikistan. Uzbekistan, where the Agency was already advising the local security services and operating some of its drones from became the turn plate of the CIA's operations in the area even though president Islam Karimov was judged as being particularly fickle and capable of expelling the American agents at any moment.

The CIA had promised that by the 23rd of September, teams would be able to land in Afghanistan in the Northern Alliance Tajiks held region. In fact, on the next Tuesday (September 25), the teams were ready but not yet in country. The reason was simple, the CIA did not wish to leave its teams acting on their own without any Special Forces support for a yet unspecified period of time. The slow delivery of the

An Mi-17 taking off, bound for Tajikistan. Officially belonging to the Northern Alliance but in fact purchased by the CIA which then handed over those aircrafts to the Afghan opposition, several such Mi-17 had been bought from the Russians in 2000. They gave the Northern Alliance a small but serviceable helicopter fleet that had been rendered even more effective by the fitting of modern Western avionics. By the end of 2001, two of those Mi-17 had been handed back to the CIA which was flying them with "Agency" crews. (Yves Debay Picture)

THE CIA'

SPECIAL OPERATION GROUP AT WAR

105

visas and licenses for all of the Agency's specialized equipments imposed by Uzbekistan and Tajikistan also caused some delays. Nevertheless, after some very high-level messages coming straight from the White House, a Mil MI-17 helicopter carrying the first SOG team under the command of Captain Gary X took off, heading for the headquarters of the Northern Alliance. The Russian built Mi-17, painted in the colours of the Northern Alliance had been secretly bought by the CIA a year before and had been modernized with Western electronics and a top-notch night-vision system. Captain Gary knew Afghanistan well because, a few years before, he had been the CIA station commander in Islamabad in Pakistan. He spoke Dari and Pashtou and he was now in this helicopter carrying a heavy metal suitcase stuffed full of several million dollars. During the past years spent on the ground, he had been in regular contact with the Northern Alliance leaders who were then under the command of Massoud, and he had already personally carried several "travel bags" full of thousand of dollars to finance the Alliance's war.

Gary's mission was simple: to convince the Northern Alliance to collaborate with the American government and to prepare the ground for the arrival of the regular armed forces.

At the CIA Headquarters in Langley, his team was called NALT for Northern Afghanistan Liaison Team and its code name was Jawbrea-

ker. The Jawbreaker team was made up of ten operators, Gary being the oldest and the most experimented. His executive officer was a young SOG officer who already had spent several years in Pakistan and spoke Farsi and Dari and the rest of the team was made up of a communication expert who already had several difficult missions under his belt and a was a former SEAL Team Six member, of a former Fort Bragg "Green Beret", a SOG physician, two helicopter pilots and the MI 17 mechanic.

Three hours later, the CIA helicopter landed in Panshir near the headquarters of the now deceased Major Massoud; as soon as they were out of the chopper, the team was bundled on a lorry that headed straight for one of their host's severly guarded safe house. Around 1800, John, the commo specialist, had finished setting up his transmitters and Gary was able to send a first report stating that the team and its equipment were now all safe and ready to operate.

In the evening, Gary met the Northern Alliance head of intelligence and security and he briefed him on the "plan" of the United States: the Alliance was to mobilize all of its fighters, buy masses of weapons, ammunition, food and equipment, and, finally, it had to prepare the arrival of American forces. These forces were mostly going to be made up of Special Forces acting as liaison teams between the Alliance soldiers and US units and as Forward Air Controllers for the Coalition's

Above. During Operation Anaconda, in March 2002, a CIA M-17 helicopter, with its blades turning, lands wounded Afghans and American Special Forces soldiers at the Bagram base. SOG men are certainly in the mountains tracking "Al-Qaida" members. *(DOD Picture)*

Below. On the runway at the military airport in Bagram, far fro the other aircraft, the CIA Mil MI-17 helicopters are parked in a remo spot. These machines, bought in Russia and updated with the late American technology, were used from October 2001 on f all the SOG very special missions. *(Yves Debay Pictur*

attack aircrafts in the forthcoming air campaign. In order to be take really seriously, the Jawbreaker commander also put 500 000 dolla on the bargaining table. " *And money will keep on coming"* said Gar In fact, within two weeks, no less than ten million dollars were to f low.

On the same day, in Washington, the White House experts eye were all firmly set on the south of Afghanistan where the majority the population is Pachtoun and where the Americans could count several allies among the warlords.

If, after years of covert presence and large sums of money, th situation was on the whole encouraging in that part of the country eve though the Alliance could only field less than 10 000 poorly equipe

ghters, in the South, that still was the real Taliban stronghold, it was on the other hand downright catastrophic: there was no armed opposition to speak of, only some vague intelligence gathering networks. In order to improve on that situation, the American and British decided to work together, making thus sure that their respective ressources wouldn't clash on the ground; teams penetrated in Afghanistan from neighbouring Pakistan with the specific mission of encouraging and orchestrating anti-Taliban revolts. To achieve that results, money was lavishly dished out on the warlords who agreed to join force against the Taliban and their allies. The main task of the Western agents was to sort out those warlords who were willing to join their efforts and to try to unit them with their Northern counterparts.

In the North, Gary knew that the days and even the hours were counted; on the next day, on September 27, around noon, in the heart of the Panshir valley, he met with general Mohammed Fahim, commander-in-chief of the Northern Alliance army and Doctor Abdullah Abdullah, foreign secretary. " *I have been sent here by the President of the United States, and his message to you is that American troops are going to arrive here soon ; the President counts on your cooperation*" declared Gary. "*I am in direct contact with the President and from now on, the world is looking at you! It is necessary that you mobilize all your troops and to deploy them on the front line. You will soon see what our bombers can do to the Taliban.... and here is a million dollars to begin with!*"

On October 1st, in the North of Afghanistan, a second CIA team arrived "in-country" whereas the Jawbreaker team had already split into two-man teams which had been deployed in the Takar and Kunduz areas and were already sending a steady stream of reports to Gary. "*Disciplined fighters, not enough heavy weapons, static trench warfare*". From the South, on the other hand, came the confirmation that the resistance to the Taliban amounted to almost nothing and this report caused some serious worries in Washington.

On October 3, while his subordinates were feeding the exact coordinates of the Taliban positions into their GPSs for future aerial bombardments, Gary, who had been looking for an area to turn into an airstrip for the CIA's planes, finally found a former British airstrip in the Gol-

A SOG operator. During the Afghan campaign, the CIA operated more openly than ever before, flying its armed drones over the area of operations or fighting alongsides SEALs, Delta Force, SAS or SBS detachments. The SOG operators attires and weapons reflect a complete ignorance of uniformity and military "spit and polish", generally incorporating a mix of military and civilian clothes with all sorts of weapons, depending on availability and tastes. This reconstruction of a SOG member wears a TAC-V1 assault vest over a US Marine Corps fleece and is armed with the "Para" version of the Minimi LMG; the secondary weapon is an M-9 pistol.

bahar area. As those preliminary events were unfolding, at the same moment, in Tampa, Florida, where CENTCOM the central American command is located, the commander of the CIA's special operations met general Franks, commander of CENTCOM for the first time. With the help of a few maps, he indicated the general the positions of the CIA teams, the possible points of entry for the Special Forces and he ended up with a complete situation update, giving the capabilities of every CIA agent in Afghanistan. Such a complete briefing is indeed a rare occurence but the boss of special operations had received specific instructions from Langley; he was to give general Franks a complete brief because this time, SOG teams were going to work for the benefit of CENTCOM.

Although it is not the CIA's favourite course of action, American special forces and CIA SOG teams had already worked together in the recent past. For example, in formerYugoslavia, CIA agents had gathered intelligence on war criminals and Special Forces had carried out their arrests.

On October 10, a twelve-man Special Forces A-Team was in Tajikistan, ready to be operationaly deployed into Afghanistan. On October 11, whereas Gary's team was operating in the northeast, another of the CIA's SOG team was getting ready to cross into Afghanistan together with a mixed team of special forces consisting of Army "Green Berets" and Air Force Combat Control Teams (CCTs). They were to link up with famous general Rachid Dostom who had been brought back to the forefront by the Americans (in fact, they only met up with him on October 16). On October 13, still flying in from Uzbekistan, another of the CIA's covert action group operating alongside a special forces unit was

helicoptered on to Ismail Khan's stronghold not far from the city of Herat, about a hundred kilometres from Iran.

At that precise moment, the American government was rightly afraid that if the situation really turned nasty, the teams on the ground would be extremly vulnerable. only about twenty people on the spot is arrested. On the other hand, the Jawbreaker team, operating alone on the ground, had to answer numerous requests coming from all sides but especially from the Air Force; the USAF wanted them to verify the exact coordinates of scores of different targets and to establish priority lists of these future targets. To make matters even more complicated, the CIA operators on the ground could only resort to Soviet-era maps which used, of course, different coordinates than the maps in use in the American forces; so, those coordinates had to be translated into a different grid system before being usable. This was not the only problem; the teams had no laser markers to "paint" the targets for the attack aircrafts and they experimented great difficulties to communicate directly with the USAF bombers. On October 16 the second covert action team entered Afghanistan with "*a lot, really a lot of money...*" and linked up with general Dostom. The mission of this team was to federate the various anti-Taliban groups around Dostom, and to find a usable airstrip as soon as possible so that the Agency cargo planes could bring in their vital weapons and ammunition loads.

On the same day, in the South of the country, the Peshawar CIA station in Pakistan reported that it had mana-

ged to contact a little known young Pachtoun leader who went by name of Hamid Karzai. The White House immediately decided to s him a CIA team, and to start airdropping weapons and different mi ry equipment for the benefit of his followers.

Finally, on Friday , October 19 at the end of evening, two MH- Pave Low helicopters landed in the Chamali plain, quite a distance fi the landing zonz initially chosen by Gary. But it didn't really matter be se this landing meant that the first Army Special Forces A-team, m up of the regulation twelve "Green Berets" and which answered to sign 555 " Triple Nickel ", was now present in Afghanistan. Every m ber of that first A-team was in charge than of no less than 150 kilo equipment, including state-of-the-art tactical laser designators which w going to litteraly change the face of this war . The CIA, and especiall SOG component, could now breath much more easely.

At the same moment, a force consisting of Rangers, Delta and S cial Forces operators did a show of force and seized, after a combat ju followed by a heliborne assault, a series of buildings near Kando which had been used by mullah Omar.

On October 27, a third CIA team was choppered in country and ked up with warlord Attah Mohammed in his stronghold located in South of Mazar-i-Sharif. At that moment, the Jawbreaker team had be operating for a month in Afghanistan.

By November 3, the CIA could count on four covert action teams in Afc nistan. Teams Jawbreaker and Delta were working alongsides g

ahim, Alpha was with Dostom and Bravo with Attah. On the other hand, gs were not going as well with team Charlie which was still trying to be itted by Ismail Khan in the West of the country.

On November 12, the Northern Alliance was already in control of e than half of Afghanistan while three days previously, less than 15 % he country was under their influence. The CIA teams, operating with r Special Forces comrades were now charging towards the South, e even reaching Kabul. On November 25, in the North of the coun- during the Qali-i-Jangi prison uprise, the Agency was going to lose irst covert operator, Johnny " Mike " Spann from Alpha team. On ember 7, the Taliban stronghold of Kandahar fell. After the fall of city, the main combat operations mostly took place in the mountains r Tora Bora, where two CIA teams took part in the searches of the erground networks where, according to the Afghans, Oussama Ben en was hiding. Thoses searches remained fruitless.

On February 5, 2002 in the morning, in the vicinity of the city of Gar- , east of Afghanistan and about sixty kilometres from Pakistan, und twenty SOG and special forces operators had gathered. There a helicopter behind them, and in front of them was a small stone n on which an American flag was flying. Inside the cairn was a piece ne of the New York Twin Towers. For those operators, it was mission omplished.

To topple the Taliban regime, the White House only had had to deploy CIA Special Operations Group operators. A splendid victory for such nall band of warriors.

The CIA has set up one of its camp in Afghanistan in Tarakhêl, a dozen kilometres North-West of Kabul. The camp is discreet and it has been modernized in order to shelter some of the Agency's equipment and vehicles in Afghanistan as well as the training areas for Afghan field Agents. American Agents are spread among different locations, mostly in Kabul. *(Christophe Roussel Picture)*

Right. Made famous by the different TV reports on the battle of Qala-i-Jangi in November 2001, "Dave", the surviving CIA Agent, exits the fortress while different Coalition SF operators join in the fight. Johnny Michael Spann, his CIA team mate, had no such luck, being killed by the Taliban prisoners in the first minutes of the uprising. *(Jumbish-i-Mili Picture)*

CIA Commando, March 2002.
During *Operation Anaconda*, joint US Special Forces/SOG teams scoured the mountains searching for "Al Qaida" gunmen. Many of the SOG members taking part in this operation were snipers like this reconstruction equipped with an SR-16; this operator is the observer of another SOG sniper armed with a full-bore sniping rifle. The "uniform" is typical of the SOG; mountain boots, denim trousers and fleece jacket. The radio is a PRC-128 used for ground-to-air liason and inter-unit liaison during ground operations.

SUCCESS FOR THE CIA'S UAVs

The CIA always has had a soft spot for manned and unmanned aircrafts. Even before the USAF, it fielded and flew the General Atomic Gnat 750, taking it into operational areas (Bosnia, 1995) long before its rival USAF colleagues did. A little latter, the Agency bought the stretched and armed version of this UAV, the now famous Predator. In the CIA version, this UAV is generally fitted with two Hellfire anti tank missiles and once again, the Agency was the first to use a UAV as an offensive platform, outperforming the USAF a second time.

Afghanistan gave the CIA a golden opportunity to try and test all the possible uses of the UAVs. From armed reconnaissance to intelligence gathering and bomb damage assessment, those unmanned platforms gave sterling services during the campaign.

The shooting down of a Gnat UAV on September the 22nd shed some light on the fact that the agency was already very busy in the neighbouring countries; The Taliban exposed the wreck of this aerial vehicle in Kabul but this was of course not enough to stop an effort which had started almost a year before with the deployment of UAVs in Uzbekistan. Even they operated under a thick veil of secrecy, it is known that those drones had already logged hundreds of flying hours when the war started in Afghanistan.

Under media scrutiny

The first operation involving UAVs that really caught the attention of the world press was the failed insertion and aborted extraction of Pachtoun warlord Abdul Haq in October 2001. Trying to convince his fellow tribesmen to join in the fight against the Taliban, he was betrayed, hunted down in spite of Predator air sup-

Previous pages.
Starting more than a year before the beginning of air operations over Afghanistan, the CIA fielded several I-Gnat and Predator drones from different ex-Soviet air bases located in Central Asia.
Able to loiter for more than 40 hours, the Predators are an excellent tool to locate and track Talibans
(USAF Picture)

Above, from left to right.
One of the main technical breaktrough achieved by the CIA during the conflict was the fitting of two AGM-114 Hellfire missiles on to the Predator. With an 8 kilometres range, the Hellfire can engage static or moving targets. When used in its reconnaissance role, the Predator is fitted with an AN/ZPQ-1 radar which has a 30 centimetres resolution at 10 kilometres or a one metre resolution at 28 kilometres. On a one hour mission , a Predator can thus cover a 100 square kilometres zone with its maximal resolution.
(USAF Picture)

Rig...
On an advanced base in Pakistan, a technical team prepa... an RQ-1L Predator drone before a surveillance mission over Afghanista...
(USAF Pictu...

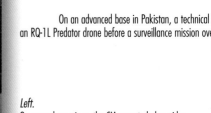

Left.
On several occasions, the CIA operated alongside the Air Force's 57th Wing Operations Group in order to undertake armed reconnaissance missions from different Middle East bases. In spite of that cooperation in the field, the Pentagon was never satisfied with the freedom of action the CIA enjoyed when it came to defining and engaging its different targets.
(USAF Picture)

The Predator B drone

The first flights of the General Atomics Tier I date back to 1989. The CIA used it quite extensively over Yugoslavia from 1994 on from air strips located in Croatia and Albania. The Tier II version brought several improvements in terms of range and payload thanks to a new, more powerful Rotax engine. Fitted with a GPS and with a sensor suite that includes two colour cameras and a thermal camera accommodated in an under fuselage Versatron / Wescam Skyball turret as well as a synthetic aperture Northrop Grumman ZPQ-Tesar radar, the Predator is certainly the most successful operational drone of the American inventory. The extensive use of those UAVs (25 000 flying hours) over the Balkans and Middle East allowed the American command to collect sensitive information which could be analysed in real time.

Some experts estimate that the different American services (CIA, US Air Force, US Navy) currently field up to 72 of those drone and that orders for several others are under way.

Even though their successes were kept quiet, General Atomics has recently revealed the existence of the B version of the Predator drone. Predator B is a much bigger and much heavier UAV than the previous Tier II version. In that updated version, an Allied Signal 331-10 turboprop replaces the Rotax engine in order to cope with the heavier weight. The operational environment (the ground station for example) and logistics of Predator B will be equivalent to that of the Tier II, and it has been designed to be easily air portable in its containers by standard C-130.

Characteristics (Tier II)

Span: 19,5 m (14,63 m).
Length: 10,36 m (8,23 m).
Weight: 2 903 kg (1 043 kg).
Autonomy: 24 hours (40 hours).
Cruising altitude: 13 700 m (7 600 m).
Payload: 295 kg (204 kg).
Speed: 210 knots (118 knots).

port he had managed to call with his satellite telephone and finally never managed to catch up with the CIA helicopter that had been sent to extract him.

On the other hand, on November 16, 2001, a CIA Predator scored a direct hit on a building sheltering "Al-Qaida" leaders after having tracked them with its on board camera. The CIA team in charge of operating that particular UAV deemed it more suitable to use the drone's Hellfire missiles rather than to wait for a latter air strike by a Navy F/A-18. Still in November, another Predator crashed when it hit a mountain side in severe weather conditions.

On January 22, 2002, an RQ-1 Predator drone crashed in Pakistan during an intelligence gathering mission over the Tribal Zone. The Pentagon refused to confirm that information or the origin of the wrecked UAV.

Cash for corpses

On February 4, 2002, a CIA Predator UAV fired two missiles at what its operators thought was a building sheltering Taliban leaders having a meeting. In fact, the three victims were identified as scrap metal collectors. In compensation, the CIA awarded each family 1000 dollars for the loss of their relatives.

Several other non attributed "strikes from the sky" were later in the campaign blamed on the CIA by the Air Force and other services that had to observe with bewilderment the fall of various munitions in their areas of responsibility they never had requested or asked for. If the CIA had agreed to lift the veil of secrecy that covers its ground actions in order to "de-conflict" them with other Special Forces, they had refused to do so for the air operations with those sometimes surprising results.

Above.
Thanks to a powerful telephoto lens, but also because it was present at the right time, a reporter managed, on January the 21st, 2002, to surprise a group of operators of the very secret Canadian group Joint Task Force Two JTF-2), leaving a USAF CH-53 with Taliban prisoners who had just been arrested. This photography forced the Canadian government to recognize the presence of this special unit in Afghanistan.
(Mario Lopes-Mills/AP/SIPA-Press Picture)

Opposite. Even though the ultra-secret JTF2 unit hardly worked "officially" with the regular tactical group units deployed by the coalition forces, some of its men worked as "terrorism counselors" with combat groups in the field. Here, soldiers from Princess Patricia's Canadian Light Infantry (PPCLI) make their way through the mountains along the Pakistan border.
(Canadian Armed Forces Picture)

Opposite right. A PPCLI combat group has just been dropp
as the Chinook takes off in a cloud of dust. These men are leavi
on patrol for several days in southeastern Afghanistan and will join
with American Special Force
(Canadian Armed Forces Pictur

At the end of January 2002, the Canadian Defence Minister, Arthur Eggleton, was criticized for not having warned Jean Chrétien, the Prime Minister as well as the Canadian Parliament that Canadian Special Forces had been deployed in Afghanistan and had taken part in several offensive operations.

This wave of indignation was started by the publication of a picture taken on Kandahar's airport tarmac on January 21, 2002, that showed elements of JTF 2, the very secretive Canadian anti-terrorist unit, escorting Taliban or "Al-Qaida" prisoners out of a US HH-53 helicopter while the Canadian government had previously declared that only regular Canadian soldiers were fighting in Afghanistan.

This debate did not concern the Canadians' presence as such, it dealt more with the fact that prisoners were going to be handed to American forces and that US authorities refused to recognize them as prisoners of war. Members of parliament and defenders of human rights protested against these actions and against the possible ill treatment of these prisoners by US troops, something the Canadian government would be, in their eyes, guilty of in collusion. Against this outcry, the Defence Minister declared first that he only had learnt of the presence of the Canadian commandos four days before; then, under media pressure, he admitted that he, in fact, had known about it for a week. Before concluding that, any way, "*their special forces respected international laws*".

A strong tradition of autonomy

While the debate raged on, Canadian Special Forces continued to operate in the South of Afghanistan with their American counterparts. JTF 2 sent, from December 2001 onwards, about thirty operators out of the 150 to 200 who are making up this unit. They were all equipped like their US colleagues in order to blend in with them during the operations.

It is noteworthy that JTF 2, which is headquartered near Ottawa, had already been deployed in Bosnia in 1994, when Serbian forces had taken Canadian soldiers hostages. However, this anti-terrorist unit had not been given the authorization to intervene.

JTF 2 teams never had to operate with the 3rd battalion of the Princess Patricia's Canadian Light Infantry (3 PPCLI) tactical groups during *Operation Apollo* - 3 PPCLI worked with the 187th Brigade Combat Team of the US Army. On the other hand, JTF 2 was always under Canadian national command (ELC), which was then located in the American headquarters on Mac Dill AFB, in Tampa, Florida. The ELC insured the liaison between the Canadian Chief of Staff in Ottawa and the American command responsible for the operations and the tasking of the various Canadian units deployed on the ground. However, in reality, JTF 2 teams operated almost completly independently, only reporting to this command after having completed their missions.

THE COVERT ACTIONS OF CANADIAN SPECIAL UNITS

A new Long Range Sniping Record

A new world-record for long-range sniping has been established by Canadian snipers in Afghanistan. A sniper pair, reinforced by US Army Sergeant Zevon Durham and using a Mc Millan .50 calibre rifle managed to hit at the second try an "Al-Qaida" member who was 2,430 metres away from its firing position.

The first .50 calibre round hit the rucksack of an unsuspecting gunman who was walking on a road in the Shah-e-Kot valley; after some adjustments, the second round found its mark, killing him instantly. The previous "record" was held by the late Gunnery Sergeant Carlos Hathcock who, thirty-five years ago while deployed to Vietnam, had killed a Viet-Cong who was 2,250 metres away from his position.

According to some specialists, the Canadian snipers are rumoured to have killed around twenty Taliban during *Operation Anaconda*. Dressed in British desert DPM clothing in order to blend in better with their surrounding, they numbered no more than five and operated in two pairs. Their skills and successes in eliminating threatening Taliban and "Al Qaida" positions made them particularly popular amongst American units which operated with them.

Left and bottom.
Just like their southern neighbours, the Canadians have a long, if discreet, tradition of sniping. The American command, well aware of their capabilities, specifically asked the Canadian government for the deployment of several sniper teams amongst Coalition combat units. The campaign proved beyond any doubts the quality of the Canadian snipers who not only managed to eliminated several dozens enemy gunmen but also established a new world record for long-range sniping when they killed an enemy at 2,430 metres with a .50 calibre rifle.
(Canadian Armed Forces Pictures)

Next sprea
A few weeks after the fall of the Taliban regim
and the rout of its last "conventional" unit
the American command decided it was tim
for the Special Forces to give way to conventional force
The SF units were then often limited to accompanyir
or providing reconnaissance to line units with
the constraining frame of conventional operatior
For JTF2 operators, the missions remained most
unchanged as its main mission remained the captu
of the most wanted terrorists but for units lik
the 3rd Battalion of the PPCLI pictured here it mea
many search and destroy operatior
in hard-to-access arec
(Canadian Armed Forces Picture

Although it is very likely that the exact figures will never be published, some experts have guessed that at least 80 % of the active duty SAS and SBS, participated, from the beginning of October 2001, in various operations in Afghanistan. According to some sources, SAS and SBS were the first to be secretly landed on Afghan soil, at the same time as CIA agents.

Others mention the possible secret presence of about twenty SAS/SBS alongside troops of the Northern Alliance. Divided into several teams, they were quickly joined by another SBS group coming from Oman. From Tajikistan, this group brought with them their white painted "NGO style" Land Rover, contrarily to the American elements which favoured locally purchased Japanese 4 X 4 vehicles.

On the Qala-e-Jangi's ramparts

Very active during operations in the North of Afghanistan, and often seen by reporters on different roads around Mazar-e-Sharif, the SAS presence was made all the more obvious from the 25th to the 27th of November 2001 during the bloody battle for the recapture of the Qala-e-Jangi fort which had fallen into the hands of former Taliban and foreign Moslem fighters who had been improperly searched after their capture (see boxed text on page 32).

SAS and SBS operators were caught on TV trying to help other US operators rescue two CIA agents who were trapped inside the fallen enclave. In November 2001, the SBS were in charge of the protection of general Tommy Franks, during his visit to Afghanistan. And on December 2, 2001, the American secretary of Defence, Donald Rumsfeld, officially praised the role of British Special Forces, assuring that they were the best in the world.

Having operated in liberated Kabul, they then headed for Kandahar with CIA agents and US Special Forces. Meanwhile, on November 15, several C-130 Hercules belonging to N°47 Squadron did a Tactical Air Landing Operation on Bagram's airport, to the utter bewilderment of the local commanders of the Northern Alliance who had not been notified of such an action by the British. After about twenty SBS had disembarked, the situation went sour between the Afghans and the British, provoking a political crisis between the Alliance and London, the British being finally obliged to leave their sup commandos stranded in one of the airport's hangar until the Afghans calmed down.

The clearing up of "Al-Qaida's" camps.

Right after the announcement of the fall of Kandahar, December 7, 2001, SAS and US green berets took charge the protection of the new temporary Afghan president, Ham Karzaï. From then on, an SAS team and a Land Rover as w as a dozen American SF operators were to be seen in front his new house.

At the same time, several teams belonging to the 22nd S Regiment were doing a recce on a camp not far from Kho

(1) N°47 Squadron is equipped with C1 / C3 Hercules C-130 and operates from the major RAF base of Lyneham. The unofficial mot of the squadron is "Sans Peur" (Without Fear), in French.

On Sunday November 25, 2001 several white painted SBS Land Rovers each mounting a GPMG on the roof are seen heading towards the Qala-e-Jangi prison, near Mazar-e-Sharif, in order to assist the Americans in the suppression of the Taliban riot and to save a CIA agent who was still trapped inside the fortress.
(Jim Hollander Photo)

At Zero Alpha, the British forces operations centre in the North of London in Great Britain, the Permanent Joint Headquarters (PJHQ) followed this operation directly. At any time, if necessary, PJHQ could alert the Defence Secretary Geoff Hoon. But the SAS did not need any other directives; they finally managed to penetrate into the various tunnels. The dust was so thick that they had to wear respirators. All the "shadows" in front of them were systematically taken down, and each of the rooms was dealt with with a hand grenade. Two other SAS were also wounded in the process of clearing up the cave complex.

Four hours later, the tunnels were cleared. The final count is self-explanatory: eighteen Afghans and foreign volunteers were dead against four wounded SAS operators. Several dozens "Al-Qaida" terrorists are lying face down, some wounded, their hands tied in their back, waiting for the American helicopters that will bring them towards a detention centre and interrogation. Some, their face in the dust, still have the force to implore for

their life, persuaded that the British are there to execute them.

The four wounded SAS were quickly evacuated towards Bagram, where one of them had to be operated directly on the spot and, regrettably, lost a leg. They were then transferred to Great Britain, by a special flight, and treated in a military hospital in Birmingham.

Beginning in February 2002, a second detachment arrived which replaced the first SAS detachment. It was high time for the "old timers" because they were starting to feel the strain of months of non-stop combat operations. For the newcomers, operations resumed on a high tempo, especially since the troops of the Northern Alliance had been side lined in favour of regular Coalition units. While they pursued "Al-Qaida" groups in the South of Afghanistan, American Delta Forces elements and CIA agents patrolled "*on the other side*", in Pakistan. Although London and Washington refused to confirm it, the SBS and the SAS conti-

OREFRONT

...at was thought to belong to "Al-Qaida". The operation was ...nder the command of the Directorate Special Forces (DSF) in ...e UK. On the ground, the SF element was under the com-...and of an old non-commissioned officer with more than fif-...en years of service under his belt. The recces had shown that ...e enemy had placed listening posts along the likely avenues ...f approaches and, for more than half an hour, SAS snipers ...ept them in their line of sight, waiting for the clearance to ...ke them out. As the green light was given, the sentries were ...uickly eliminated; white phosphorous and 40 mm grenades ...ere hurled directly into the caves openings. For a few seconds, ...ere was only noise and dust, while SAS operators were trying ...o rush inside the various tunnels dug by the Taliban in the ...ountain. Although shaken by the explosions, the occupants ...f the tunnels reacted very quickly and fired all their weapons, ...ainly AK-47s, before peeling back into the depths of the tun-...els. Two SAS were wounded during the attack, one of whom, ...riously wounded in the abdomen and in the leg, fell uncon-...ious at the scene.

British SBS during the Bagram tactical air landing operation on November the 15th 2001. The uniform worn by this operator is closer to British Army regulations than the weird combinations previously sported by the SAS. The mix of a desert DPM trousers with a temperate DPM Kit Carry Smock was found to be very effective on the Afghan theatre of operations. A desert DPM bush hat and the ubiquitous Shemagh complete the uniform of this SBS. The weapons are the regulation Browning L9 preferred over the SIG P226 and P228 that are also used by the British SF and the SA80 rifle, preferred over the Diemaco C8 (a Canadian built version of the M4) that is standard issue to the British Special Forces. An Arktis chest rig is used to carry additional magazines and the rest of the equipment is to be found in the cavernous Saracen "bergen" carried by this soldier.

nued, in April 2002, to work alongside the Royal Marine of 45 Commando. It is certain that their number had by then been greatly reduced: around thirty altogether which is not much when compared to the one thousand seven hundred Royal Marines of 3 Commando Brigade who were then deployed on the ground. At this point, the SAS / SBS missions were not offensive any more; they essentially consisted in recce operations along the border with Pakistan. Naturally, these actions revolved around the search for Ben Laden and his lieutenants who were rumoured to enjoy relative freedom of movement in the border Tribal areas.

At that period, the main problems facing Brigadier Lane, commander of 3 Commando Brigade, was to find targets justifying operations on a large scale without incurring too much media flak!

The anti "Al Qaida" maritime operations.

From the end of September, 2001 British and American intelligence services had set up a "naval hunting plan" and, in mid-December US Navy and Royal Navy vessels chased about twenty different vessels suspected of having links with the terrorist group of Ben Laden. Aboard each of the British warships, teams of SBS were ready to "take down" any vessel belonging to what the Pentagon grandly called the " terrorist fleet ", which was rumoured to be capable of transporting weapons, explosives or substances capable of contaminating the "infidels".

Naturally, western security services turned first and foremost to Panamanian, Liberian or Cyprian vessels that are known to be lax with international law. An enormous amount of research was carried out in just a few weeks in order to compile a huge database on the thousand of vessels that are steaming daily around the globe and that could, in one guise or another, pose a threat. About twenty ships were "selected", of which the first was the MV NISHA, intercepted on December 21, 2001 by an SBS assault team off the Southern coast of Great Britain. The vessel had left Sandown's bay opposite the Isle of Wight and navigated under the Saint-Vincent Grenadines' pavilion (this Caribbean island state has, for a population of under 120 000, more than 1 300 boats flying its colours!). Its cargo was some unrefined sugar bound for the Port of London, and had to sail past the highest building in the British capital, the very symbolic Canary Wharf already targeted by PIRA in the 90s. Information originating from an allied foreign service made it plausible that the MV Nisha could be transporting explosives. The complete search of the vessel undertaken by the SBS accompanied by policemen from the London Metropolitan Police Special Branch did not produce anything, but it confirmed the experts' fears, namely the vulnerability of the targets bordering the Thames in London. Following this operation, the British union of sea transports demanded the measure that was already in effect in the USA (a ninety-six hours waiting period in front of the harbour before a vessel can moor and land its goods, and the advance dispatch to the port of disembarkation of the complete list of the crew) be introduced in the UK. Since then, dozens of such VBSS (Visit Board Secure Seize) operations have been undertaken by the SBS, but also by American SEALs, Australian SBS and French Commando-Marine on all the potentially dangerous sea lanes but so far without any results.

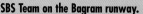
British commandos boarding a Chinook HC-2 at the start of a night time insertion into Taliban country. SBS and SAS remained "in country" alongside other conventional British units until the summer of 2002. Their missions were varied, ranging from long range reconnaissance patrols to night time ambush around Coalition bases in order to try and eliminate remaining Taliban and "Al-Qaida" members. *(MOD Picture)*

SBS Team on the Bagram runway.
On November 15, 2001, SBS fighters surrounded the Bagram airfield. Their dress is more official than that of their SAS counterparts : DPM desert camouflage pants and a DPM Kit Karry Smoke jacket. A mixture of forest and desert camouflages turned out to be very effective in the Afghan terrain. The desert Bonnie Hat and the regimental Shemag complete the outfit. Even though the regularly used guns are the SIG P226 and P228, some men still prefer the Browning GP PA carried in a hip holster. It's the same with the assault rifles : the SA80 is the choice here, rather than the Diemaco C8, the Canadian version of the M4, standard equipment in the British Special Forces. An Arktis Chest Webbing is used for carrying additional ammunition. Personnel items, rations and medicine are carried in the impressive Saracen back packs.

Modest results

In the end of April, 2002, the British staff decided to de the terrorist movements a big blow and to deploy more the a thousand soldiers, almost all Royal Marines, in *Operation S* *pe.* Announced on May the 2nd - although it had begun fo days before-this operation, which took place in the southec of Afghanistan about fifty kilometres from Khost, consisted hunting down the last "Al-Qaida" fighters and in destroyi their mountain weapons and ammunition stores. Air reco naissance showed suspect movements that could mean that important number of Taliban and "Al-Qaida" fighters were s hiding in the mountains. According to London, it was the mo important military operation since the First Gulf War. It is tr that the full potential of the rifle companies of 45 Comman was thrown into the operation; it was supported by all of t RAF's available Chinook helicopters, the 105 mm Light Gu of 29 Commando Regiment Royal Artillery, Royal Enginee sappers, US Army Apache helicopters and USAF A-10. The S and the SAS were also of course part of this operation. Th were inserted ahead of the main force and they secured a nur ber of cliff tops in order to prevent any escape by enemy fo ces that would trying to escape from the Royal Marine Con mandos.

Brigadier Roger Lane, Royal Marine, thus presented th operation; "*The zone has never been recced by the Coaliti forces and we have good reason to think that there is a ve*

SAS trooper operating in the East of Afghanistan at the end of 2001.

On the 18th of December, a joint SAS/SBS patrol is searching the Tora-Bora mountains. At that point in the conflict, the British are not convinced that the pro-governmental Afghan troops are really willing to fight and they prefer to undertake those search and destroy missions themself. The cold being bitter at that time of the year in the Afghan mountains, this trooper wears a fleece and cut down gloves. During this operation which was commanded directly from the UK, the British special operators assaulted a cave complex and cleared it with clock work precision in spite of a very high volume of Taliban fire that cost them two wounded.

SBS operator during the Qala-i-Jangi uprising, November 2001. During the Qala-i-Jangi jail siege, the SBS came to the rescue of their American Special Forces colleagues on November the 25th and managed to save a CIA agent that had been trapped in the fortress. Another CIA field agent was not so lucky and he was killed by the rioting prisoners. During that action, the SBS were sporting purely civilian clothes, offering a very different appearance from their Bagram arrival barely ten days before. The "long" (SAS slang for a rifle) is a canadian Diemaco C8. The Shemagh and the DPM pattern holster for the SIG P226 are the only giveaway that this operator is actually British.

important "Al-Qaida" base in the vicinity, given that, due to the strategic location of this area, the enemy can operate on the four cardinal points." However, at the conclusion of the operation, to justify this operation in the wake of innumerable press attacks which sneered at the small number of enemy killed, Brigadier Lane insisted on the fact that this operation was not to be evaluated in terms of terrorist bodies, *"but in the destruction of "Al-Qaida's" infrastructure"*. After the mixed results of the Tora Bora operations, the small results of *Operation Anaconda* around Gardez, American general Tommy Franks, commander of the Coalition forces in Afghanistan, decided to trust this new operation to the British only, with a symbolic Afghan presence. (It is necessary to say that the Afghan allies had a very bad name with the Coalition staff, being accused of having let Ben Laden run away with hundreds of his fighters during the offensive against the Tora Bora massif in December 2001.)

Six camouflaged Chinook took off from Bagram in the dark of night to land on two advanced bases near Khost. Inside the

---

(2) In the morning of May the 23rd, there was however an exchange of shots when a lookout of the Brigade Recce Force Royal Marine was fired on by an automatic weapon near Khost, by gunmen who had disembarked from two vehicles. The Royal Marines managed to kill two of them whose bodies were recovered by the aggressors before they ran away. Immediately afterwards, two stand-by French Air Force Mirage 2000 were called in to chase after these vehicles, but without result.

win rotor helicopters were the SBS and SAS teams and an dvanced detachment of the Brigade Recce Force. Three hours ter, still at night, the first teams were helicoptered into the fghan mountains and began their movement: Qperation Sni- e had started.

Sixteen days later, the operation was over and there was ery little to show for it. Nevertheless, the start had been auspi- ous. A column of Australian SAS, made up of light 4 x 4 and x 6 vehicles had been attacked at 2 AM by Taliban who had anaged to put together a real ambush with 120 mm mortar unds, RPG-7s and heavy machine guns. At dawn, an AC-130 ectre " Gunship " had come to the rescue to crush the aggres- rs. The Coalition staff were expecting a strong enemy pre- nce. But, very quickly, Royal Marine and Special Forces noti- d that they were only confronting thin air; and, instead of e discovery and destruction of stockpiles of terrorist wea- ns, the British had to admit they only found some ware- ouses belonging to a local warlord that had been filmed two onths before by journalists! The Royal Marine commander as then forced to admit that there had been no contacts with e enemy (2), the only "losses" being SAS and staff of the 32 eld Hospital who had been contaminated by a particularly silient form of diahorea!

The American command had maybe forgotten a little too uickly the nature of Afghanistan, an immense country, with very difficult geography, where communications are limited some dirt tracks and roads and to satellite telephones. And at contacts with the enemy-when they happen- tend to take ace in some of the world's most remote areas!

sychological operations

At the beginning of June, the British units launched another eration along the border with Pakistan, to try and cut "Al- aida" lines of communication with the hinterland and to pre- ent terrorists disrupting the Loya Jirga, the traditional mee- ng of Afghan leaders. They then had to operate in a zone that ad been fiercely bombarded during the previous *Operation*

Top of the previous page.
RAF Chinooks played a crucial role during the campaign, ferrying men and equipments accross the areas of operation. T he covert presence of SAS/SBS teams among the ranks of Northern Alliance troops and in the South of Afghanistan was reported as early as the end of September 2001; in the North of the country, the British operators brought with them from Tajikistan some of their "NGO style" white painted Land Rovers.
(MOD Picture)

Right.
Tora-Bora region, December 2001. This M4 SOPMOD armed British SAS/SBS operators has just debussed from a vehicle and he is heading towards the area of operations alongsides Northern Alliance soldiers. After the Tora-Bora failure and the lackluster results of *operation Anaconda* in the Gardez region, General Franks, overall commander of Coalition troops in Afghanistan, decided to only trust operations to the American or the British, with nothing more than a symbolic Afgfhan presence.
(Roméo Gacad/AFP Picture)

Below.
On the Bagram airfield, a group of British SBS chats with American Special Forces operator who have just landed in their Chinook. On the 15th of November 2001, around twenty SBS did a tactical air landing operation on the Bagram airport and seized it, to the utmost annoyance of the Northern Alliance fighters who had not been warned of such an operation and who were not amused at the British intrusion on their territory.
(Getty/SIPA-Press Picture)

To arrest the traitors to Her Majesty

Alongside some SAS and SBS operations that were very well covered by the media, the British government also decided to send some very discreet MI5 and MI6 teams on the ground in Afghanistan and in Pakistan. The mission of these teams was to interrogate the members of the "Al-Qaida" network of British origin arrested in these two countries. Several elements were thus identified, including a Scotsman converted to Islam, who went by the name of James McLintock and who was in Pakistani custody. When they arrived "in country" MI5 possessed a list of about two hundred names of Moslem fighters and holders of British passports who had left Great Britain in the past few years to train and to fight in Afghanistan and in Chechnya. However, they also knew that an unspecified number of them had already got back to the UK when operations began in October 2001.

Since the end of the war, MI5 and MI6 officers have spent hundred of hours interrogating everyone who could be considered as being connected in some way to the UK and they spent countless hours poring over documents left by the Taliban and "Al-Qaida" members in order to try and reconstruct the terrorist network and its possible branches in Great-Britain.

the city of Mazar-e-Sharif who were fighting over the contr of the police stations. The presence of Occidental soldiers was sufficient to defuse a potentially dangerous confrontation. War seemed to be never ending for the special forces of Her Majesty!

Series of pictures taken on Tuesday the 18th of December 2001 in th White Mountains near Tora-Bora in the East of Afghanistan. A SAS/SB patrol has just left its vehicle and is now heading for the mountain top to start a "recce". Only a single member of this patrol carries a heavy "bergen". At that very moment, the British were having serious doubts on the fighting spirit of the pro-governmental Afghan soldiers against the "Al-Qaida" members and decided to see for themselves what the situation on the ground really was like.
(David Guttenfelder/AP/SIPA-Press Picture)

Buzzard, an area of strongly divided tribes. At first, several recce teams, made up of a mix of SAS and SBS operators, searched the hills along the neighbouring Pakistani border, followed in the valleys by light vehicles. This time, the British were going to try and combine their military operation with psychological actions, in order to win " hearts and minds " and gather information that could help locate Taliban and " Al-Qaida " members. The information which resulted from this operation was that the Islamist fighters had disappeared from those mountains and crossed into Pakistan a month ago.

On June 10, a strong party of Royal Marines and SBS was sent ahead of a detachment of a hundred and twenty American Special Forces operators who surrounded the village of Alatay, in the South of Afghanistan. There, they discovered four hides and arrested seventeen people suspected of belonging to "Al-Qaida" or of being sympathizers of this terrorist organization. In the hides, the Coalition soldiers found weapons, explosives, bomb making equipment and documents. This raid had been triggered by hard intelligence. Ten days later, in the village of On Wipan, about twenty kilometres of Khost, Royal Marines, together with SBS operators, discovered a stockpile of weapons amounting to five truckloads; they decided to destroy the older weapons and to give the other ones to the new Afghan army.

On July 11, a team made up of British and American SF intervened between the units of generals Dostom and Atta, in

SAS trooper in the Tora-Bora region in December 2001.
The SAS also took part in some high altitude anti-terrorits search operations during their Afghanistan deployment, particularly in December 2001, in the Tora-Bora region. During that specific operation, the "uniform of the day" was a mix of military and civilian clothing and equipments, the main weapon remaining, as now usual for British SF operators, the canadian made Diemaco C8.

"AL-QAIDA'S" TRACKS

An australian 6X6 LRPV in the South of Afghanistan. Mountain operations and severe weather conditions could have posed a serious challenge to those troops for whom operations in humid tropical or sub-tropical environment are the norm; Only C Mountain Troop receives mountain training in the South-East of Australia and in New-Zealand. *(ADF Picture)*

Above.
One of the Special Task Force Group 6X6 recce vehicle crossing a river during *Operation Slipper*. The ring mounted .50 calibre HMG has been removed in order to improve the load carryiong capability of this particular vehicle.

Following page, top.
Near Bagram, one of the SAS' vehicle patrolling a zone known to be often infiltrated byTaliban fighters. During the war, the SFTG operated alongsides American Special Forces and British SAS, all units using very similar equipment and procedures.

Following page, bottom.
Range practise for Australian SAS near Bagram. All those operators are using Colt M4s (one being also fitted with an M203); The operations in Afghanistan gave the vivid proof that this short assault rifle is in the process of replacing the HK MP5 as the Special Forces' weapon of choice.

Left.
Since Australia does not own any super heavy lift aircrafts, the ADF had to resort to the renting of some Antonov An-124 from a specialized Ukrainian company. Those huge aircrafts flew the SAS' heavy equipment (including their 6x6 and 4x4 vehicles) towards the Middle East while the SAStroopers were flown in by the RAAF own jets.
(ADF Pictures)

On December 3, 2001, Australian Defence Minister Rob Hill officially announced that *Operation Slipper* had starte The elite of the Australian armed forces, an SAS detachme of unspecified strength, was to be deployed to Afghanistan help in the fight against terrorism.

On the very same day, an SAS advanced party landed US Marine Corps Camp Rhino airstrip, South of Kandahar. T days later, the one hundred and fifty operators strong recei ly formed Special Force Task Group (STFG) had reached its f complement and was ready to start operating.

Having been flown in by Antonov 124 from Perth with th 6 x 6 and 4 x 4 vehicles, the SAS first landed in Kuwait order to be joined by some of their companions arriving fro Diego Garcia. They were then transported in theatre by C-13

Search and deep recce operations

The SAS mission in Afghanistan was going to consist of hu ting down remaining Taliban and "Al-Qaida" groups and performing long range reconnaissance missions in support the Coalition. The Australian SAS proved to be particularly a at both tasks, something that was to come brilliantly to lig during *Operation Anaconda*.

The Special Task Force Group consisted of a reinforced squ dron numbering at least ninety operators probably divide into four officers and sixty other ranks, plus a command an control and support (transport, medical, transmissions an logistics) elements. At first, the SAS were based in Camp Rh no. Afterward, this base only served as a rear echelon, t SAS patrols being deployed on the ground.

The STFG operated with American Special Forces, US an

Above. An SAS motorized reconnaissance team includes two 6x6 Long Range Patrol Vehicles (LRPV) and a Perentie Reconnaissance Vehicle (PRSV), derived from the Series 110 Land Rover and adapted for the Special Forces. Along with the British SAS, the Australian SAS have undoubtedly the most experience in long-range desert patrols and reconnaissance, since they have trained for years in the harsh deserts of northeastern Australia. It is thus common that, during traini missions, SAS vehicles out on patrol remain in the bush several week even up to two months.

Opposite. On the Bagram airport runway on July 29, 2002. An Australian SAS group stands behind a 101st Air Assault Chinook during a pre-mission briefing. During Operation Anaconda, the Australi SAS participated in their hardest fighting since the Vietnam War, arou the towns of Marzak and Zurmat in the different valleys of Shah-e-Ko at the beginning of March, 2002.

SPECIAL AIR SERVICE REGIMENT

Opposite right. One of the most impressive views of Operation Slipp in Afghanistan. The Australian SAS are here aboard a 6x6 known a Long Range Patrol Vehicle (LRPV). Notice the weaponry on the LRP a 12.7-mm M2QCB main gun mounted on a turret and a 7.62-m MAG gun riveted out in front on the lefthand side. The LRPV is excellent vehicle, especially designed for the desert, with an elec winch to pull itself out of the sand, two centrally-located spare whee and often a motorcycle attached at the back to be used for liaiso

Following double page. Between two long-range patrol missio in eastern and southeastern Afghanistan, several SAS teams pract firing with light weapons in a remote area. Here all the SAS fight have M-4s with 40-mm grenade launche (Australian Ministry of Defense Picture

SPECIAL AIR SERVICE REGIMENT (SASR)

Created in 1957, the Australian SAS Regiment traces its roots from the Second World War M and Z independent companies. The SASR first combat operations were undertaken in 1965 against the Indonesians in Borneo.

A year later, the SASR was sent to Vietnam where it saw active service until pulled out in 1971.The awesome reputation of that unit was essentially built during that conflict when they became the Vietcong's worst nightmare, being nicknamed "the ghosts of the jungle" by their Vietnamese enemies. The SASR then had to wait for more than twenty years before being deployed again, this time to Somalia in support of the Australian infantry battalions that were opposing heavily armed militias in the streets of Mogadishu.

In September 1999, the SASR was the first Australian unit to officially penetrate into East Timor during *operation Stabilize*; officially only, because unofficially the SASR had already infiltrated several teams in East and West Timor before the beginning of military operations on the island. During the 2000 Sidney Olympic Games, the Australian government suddenly paid a lot more attention to the SASR, giving it the capability to carry out large-scale counter-terrorism missions. The SAS were showered with new equipment

and weapons in order to improve their capabilities to undertake amphibious, urban and air operations.

By the end of September 2001, an SASR squadron was already on stand-by to be deployed at a very short notice. The first SAS detachment only landed in Afghanistan on December 3, 2001.

Today, the SASR is the real backbone of the Australian Special Forces. Based in Perth, it is made up of seven hundred volunteer troopers. Before applying for selection (during which about 90 % of the candidates are weeded out),soldiers must have served several years in regular army units. The regiment has several active duty squadrons, but also several reserve units and it can also count on the support of the Army's 4 Royal Australian Regiment (Commando).

The SAS Regiment is made up of three 90-man strong "Sabre" Squadrons and a support Squadron which provides the Regiment with its medical, transportation, engineer and catering specialists. The training Squadron is organized in five different groups, each in charge of training the future SAS operators in the different skills vital to the SASR. Finally, during operational deployments, 152 Signals Squadron provides the different Sabre Squadrons with communication support.

All those squadrons are placed under the command of a regimental headquarters.

The three Sabre Squadrons live and train according to a three year cycle. The operators dedicate the first year to the mastering of new techniques and developping them. The second year is more specifically dedicated to the special missions of a squadron: reconnaissance, sabotage, intelligence gathering...during this year, the Squadron practises amphibious, air and land operations. Finally, during the third year, the squadron is the "stand-by squadron" as the national counter-terrorist team. During this year, the operators are on the alert twenty-four hours a day and they can be called up either for exercises or for real operations at any moment.

Within the SASR, every squadron specializes in a type of infiltration. They are divided between air operations (parachuting, helicopter insertion or tactical air landing), amphibious operations (small boats, submarine and canoes insertions, closed-circuit breathing apparatus) and land operations (using for example the LRPV 6 x 6 special vehicles).

Royal Marines as well as their British SAS "cousins", a unit to which the SASR is especially close to in terms of operating procedures.

The Australian SAS were deployed with their new "desert" version of the famous "jelly bean" camouflage. Their main weapons were the now classic SF armament, M-16A2, C-4 , F-89 Minimi, FN MAG, M2QCB , SR-98, and Barrett M-82 A1; the SAS were also equipped with MK-19 40 mm automatic grenade launchers, a weapon that was not then in service with the rest of the Australian armed forces.

A minimum
of three hundred enemy KIAs.

In February 2002, the SAS driver of a 6 x 6 LRPV (Long Range Patrol Vehicle), Sergeant Andrew Russell, was killed when he drove over an antitank mine. That death led a number of experts to wonder why the Australian command had not yet, like the American had already done, replaced their Special Forces by regular line units like the 101st or the 82nd Airborne or the 10th Mountain Division.

During *Operation Anaconda*, the Australian SAS took part in the most intense combat operations undertaken by Australian Forces since the Vietnam War. These actions were centred on the cities of Marzak and Zurmat and in the Shah-e-Kot valley. During the operations around Takur Ghar, on March 3 and 4, 2002, while SEALs, CCTs and Rangers were battling

around a hundred "Al-Qaida" members, several SAS took up positions on mountain ridges situated 10000 ft above sea level, in temperatures reaching nineteen degrees below zero in order to designate enemy positions to Coalition tactical air support. According to the "Aussies'" estimates, they indirectly killed more than three hundred Islamist fighters during this operation that lasted for more than ten days. After these combat operations, the SAS resumed their search operations on foot in the mountains or with their 6 x 6 Land Rovers on the plains, locating and destroying several Taliban and "Al-Qaeda" weapons caches.

A very important effort

In April 2002 another similar-sized one replaced the initial Australian SAS detachment. The Australian SAS contingent was only second in size to their British counterparts and this represents a very substantial effort for an SF unit that is only half the size of the British SAS/SBS group. At the end of August, 2002, the second detachment of Australian SAS was replaced by a third contingent which continued to operate in the same zones in the southeast of Afghanistan, hunting down the remaining "Al-Qaida" and Taliban which were intermingled and often operated together. That sort of attrition warfare is typical of guerrilla and counter-guerilla operations in which every zone must be regularly combed for mines and booby traps. An exhausting task, but an excellent war school for the Australian SAS!

The Special Task Force Group

The Special Task Force Group was composed of a reinforced squadron, that is at least ninety men : four officers and sixty men (normally), plus a command detachment and support troops (transportation, medical, transmissions and logistics). At first these troops were housed at Camp Rhino. Later this base was simply used as a rear logistics camp, and the SAS teams lived in the field.

Top left.
One of the 150 SAS members making up the second rotation group of Australian Special Forces during Operation Slipper. The quality of these elite soldiers was appreciated by the military experts who judged them second only to the British SAS/SBS in size. We are speaking of the two hundred members of Her Majesty's Special Force present in Afghanistan. The Aussies' contribution was a major one when we consider that there are twice as many British SAS/SBS fighters as there are Australian.

Above and opposite
On board a Chinook belonging to the 101st Air Assault, Australian S paratroopers are being transported to an observation post for a sho length mission. Note the length of the hair of the person sitting on t back trap door beside the machine gunne
(Australian Ministry of Defense Pictur

135

Above. At the end of August 2002, the second detachment of Australi[an] SAS soldiers was replaced by a third which continued the same work [in] the same sections of southeastern Afghanistan, relentlessly tracking t[he] "Al-Qaida" groups and the Talibans, which were often one and the sam[e]. It was a war of attrition, of guerrilla and counter-guerrilla activity, whe[re] every inch of territory had to be checked and rechecked while trying [to] avoid mines and booby-traps. Exhausting work but excellent war traini[ng] for the Australian SAS[.]

Ci-contre. Coming back from a reconnaissance mission the 6x6 and 4x4[s] are preceded by two SAS paras on an all-terrain motorcyle used for light reconnaissance in difficult terrain. Here the motorized unit is entering a village in the region around Bagram. *(Australian Ministry of Defense Pictures)*

Opposite page.
1,2. The first SAS detachment deployed in Afghanistan returning to Australia in April of 2002, where they were hailed as national heroes.
3. Army Chief of Staff Lieutenant General Peter Leahy speaking to the 150 SAS paras as they returned to Perth on August 30, 2002, after five months in Afghanistan.
4. In a village in eastern Afghanistan, a traditionally pro-Taliban zone, an Australian SAS paratrooper and his interpreter question a group of Afghans. The information gathering performed by the three successive detachments of Australians was considered by the Americans to be excellent.
6. Major General Frank "Buster" Hagenbeck, commander of Task *Force Mountain*, awards the Bronze Star to Lieutenant Colonel Rowan Tink, leader of the Australian Special Forces group, on July 16, 2002.
7. The Australian Special Air Service Regiment (SASR) furnished three groups in all during *Operation Slipper*, each successive group forming the Special Forces Task Force. Each group operated in Afghanistan for five or six months.
(Australian Ministry of Defense Pictures)

1	2
4	3
5	
6	7

Above and opposite right.
A team of Australian sailors leave their semi-rigid inflatable to board a ballaga in the Persian Gulf. Between Africa, the Arabian peninsula and Pakistan, hundreds of boats of this type transport all sorts of goods, and certainly members of "Al-Qaida".
(Australian Ministry of Defense Picture)

Opposite left.
An Australian Navy boarding team climbs onto a ship to be searched during antiterrorist operations directed against the varied and obscure "Al-Qaida" networks. Note the pump-action shotgun, an excellent weapon for use in breaking open locks on doors and lockers.
(Australian Ministry of Defense Picture)

Below.
In the Persian Gulf, a boarding team, composed of crew members of the HMS Melbourne with commando operatives discreetly mixed in, comes back after checking out a merchant ship. Note the specific equipment : helmet, life jacket, individual communications system and light clothing well adapted to the climate.
(Australian Ministry of Defense Picture)

Above top to bottom.
On board a rapid RHIB, for Rigid Hull Inflatable Boat, an inspection team composed of SAS paras and marines has just left HMAS Sydney and is heading towards a ship to undertake a search.

Opposite.
Once ships have been spotted by the vessels of the antiterrorist coalition, the various naval intervention units intercept them and do rapid searches. Here, to gain time, the Australian Navy commando ropes down from a helicopter onto boats suspected of belonging to the terrorist movement "Al-Qaida".

Above right.
On board a speed boat, a boarding team made up of eight soldiers and a pilot is preparing to leave one of the Australian ships, part of the multinational interception Force, cruising in the Indian Ocean. In all, specialized teams from the Australian Navy performed several hundred searches on boats of all shapes and sizes

Below far right.
Two teams, trained for boarding and searching ships in the Indian Ocean, ready their gear and wait for orders. One team will go out in a speed boat ; the other will board a Sea King helicopter belonging to the Australian Navy.
(Australian Ministry of Defense Pictures)

At the beginning of October, 2001, the SASR B Squadro Boat Troop embarked on HMAS Kanimbla. Besides the contr of merchant vessels in the Indian Ocean off the coasts of Paki tan, this detachment was also meant to be used in case of non-combatant evacuation operation (NEO) of Australian exp triates living in Pakistan. In case of such an eventuality, th operators could have used the RAN (Royal Australian Nav ships as command, control and logistic centres while using th onboard S-70A-9 Blackhawk for their insertions and extra tions only resorting to Pakistani airbases if necessary.

Different options had been studied for the transportation the Australian Task Force to the Afghan theatre of operations. Th speed of military operations in November, 2001, with the Tal ban defeat arriving so rapidly made the choice of an air landir operation the simplest; the American command then gave th green light for the arrival of the Australian SAS in Kandahar.

At sea, the SASR were given several opportunities to pro tise their finely-honed skills on vessels suspected of hiding "A Qaida" or of being of interest to the Coalition's Intelligen services. That sort of boarding operation was nothing new the Australian SAS who had already practised it on August 2 2001, when a detachment of about fifty SAS had seized an secured a Norwegian cargo boat named Tampa on which fou hundred and thirty eight refugees were found in very prec rious conditions. The vessel had decided to penetrate into th Australian territorial waters around Christmas Island.

THE NEW ZEALAND SAS IN ACTION

It is from a BBC telegram dated Thursday, October 25, 2001, at 3. 47 local time, that the world learnt that several New Zealand SAS teams were based on the Island of Diego Garcia in the Indian Ocean. Indeed, at the conclusion of a major exercise conducted by the British armed forces in Oman, in which several special units had taken part, the "Kiwis" had not returned to New Zealand but had instead elected to head for this island, an unsinkable RAF and USAF "aircraft carrier" stranded in the middle of the ocean.

Surrounded by the greatest secrecy, the New Zealand government had given a favourable answer to the American plea for assistance and had decided to join in the international antiterrorist coalition by committing vessels, transport aircraft and Special Forces to operations. On November 3, 2001 the Wellington government announced the presence of NZ SAS in Afghanistan as a fait accompli. This statement provoked a grave political crisis on the island that seemed to threaten to destabilize Jim Anderton, the NZ Prime Minister. This crisis was made all the worst by the fact that the Prime Minister flatly refused to communicate any information on the deployment of the NZ SAS on the ground of operational security; this refusal was extended even to the representatives of his own party. "It is a secret force and, to be effective it has to operate in secret " said Helen Clark, the New Zealand government leader .

"The best of the best "

But this attitude also caused strong attacks from the opposition who thought that the NZ SAS were not properly equipped to fight in Afghanistan. Immediately the New Zealand government and its armed forces had to clarify this issue, stating that contrary to these assertions, the detachment of the New Zealand Special Air Service (NZSAS) in Afghanistan was not ill-equipped. Nevertheless, according to the New Zealand press, the SAS have suffered from a lack of funding and appropriate equipment; on the other hand, according to various members of the government and of the Army command, who never hesitated to stand up for its SF operators, there was nothing further from the truth. Quoting a field grade officer serving in the Pentagon, the New Zealand SAS would even rank, "among the best special forces deployed on the ground".

The NZ SAS Squadron was initially formed in 1954 and operated for the first time with 22 SAS in Malaysia. Ten years later the New Zealand SAS fought in Vietnam; in 1978 the unit became the 1st SAS Squadron and in 1991 they took part in special operations in the Gulf against Iraq. Today, the NZ SAS is made

p of about a hundred and twen-
 soldiers who train regularly
ith their Australian and British
ounterparts.

n the heart
f Tora Bora

Even though, true to their stance,
e NZ government never produced any
fficial figures on the NZ involvement in
fghanistan, it is considered that the New
ealand detachment was made up of around
irty operators, most of them from
e NZ SAS, which is composed of two
quadrons. About forty SAS were left
n the national territory as a reaction
rce against possible terrorist attacks.
Contrary to what was sometimes written,
e New Zealand SAS did not operate with the Australian SAS.
e main reason for that was that the two SAS units operated
 different zones and while the NZ SAS were dependent on the
mericans units deployed in the Bagram area for their logistics

and command elements the Australians were operating
autonomously in the Kan-
dahar region.
The New Zealand
SAS operated in
Afghanistan with
their modified 4 x 4
Land Rover vehicles,
and they earnt praise for their actions
around Tora Bora towards the end of
December 2001. During this period they
operated alongside their British SAS and SBS
counterparts, like "in the good old days" of Malaysia and Iraq.

With the exception of their countrymen and a few Australians,
the world knew nothing of the New Zealand soldiers engaged
in the war in Afghanistan. *(MOD Picture)*

Altogether, fifty Jegerkommandoen and Marinekommandoen belonging to the Norwegian Special Forces were deployed in Afghanistan from January to May 2002.

Below.
A norwegian operator "painting" a Taliban target with a Litton GLTD-II laser designator for the benefit of a Coalition attack aircraft.
(Norwegian MOD pictures)

THE NORWEGIAN SPECIAL FORCES IN THE AFGHAN MOUNTAINS

At the beginning of January 2002, under strong media pressure, the spokesman of the Norwegian command, Petter Lindquist, confirmed the presence of Norwegian troops in Afghanistan, but he flatly refused to reveal their exact number. Some sources thought that the element was 70 to 80 strong. "T*he national contingent consists of Marinejegerne naval commandos from the Ramsund naval base near Harstad as well as army commandos originating from the Fallskjermjegerkommandoen. These soldiers took part in several operations and have not, to this day, suffered any casualties.* "

Indeed, during *Operation Anaconda*, the Norwegian commandos, alongside their American SEAL and German KSK colleagues, faced Al-Qaida fighters in the South of Gardez for over nine days. For the duration of that period, they benefited from around the clock air support at three minutes' notice from B-1 and B-52 bombers, F-15s, AC-130 "Gunships" and Apache helicopters. This is a luxury few countries can afford.

All services included (Navy and Army), the norwegian SF contingent only operated under the orders of Task Force K-Bar which was commanded by a Navy Special Warfare Command element. The top picture presents a norwegian commando armed with a 5,56 mm Minimi light machine gun in a lying up position (LUP) observing a zone of potential "Al-Qaida" activity; the middle picture shows a norwegian element fast roping down from an American Special Forces Chinook helicopter; the bottom picture taken from another norwegian LUP; note the Leica Geovid laser range finder and the HK USP pistol. Alongsides their Navy and Army Special Forces, the Norwegians also sent, from December 2001, a 15 man strong Explosive Ordnance Disposal team on the Kandahar airport, several liason officers teams, fifteen armoured vehicles, a C-130 Hercules based in the Manas airbase as well as some staff to the ISAF when it became operational. *(Norwegian MOD pictures)*

145

The Norwegian naval commandos

The MarineJegerne or Norwegian naval commandos can easily be compared with the British SBS or the American SEAL. All the operators of this unit are fully-trained combat swimmers and are capable of undertaking offensive missions with closed-circuit breathing apparatus. Their two main missions consist in deep recce from the sea line and in destruction and sabotage operations of vessels and naval installations. It is noteworthy that all Norwegian frogmen are HALO qualified. These commandos have a very strong ongoing link with the British SBS.

Two national contingents specialising in Arctic conditions

The Scandinavian Special Forces task force took the name of NORSOF TG and it first landed in Afghanistan discreetly during the first days of January 2002. Two contingents were going to serve in the South of Afghanistan under American command, each for a duration of three months.

According to specialists, the Americans asked the Norwegian government (which already had, in November 2001, proposed the use of their special forces) to reinforce them with units specialized in arctic warfare. Given the geographic situation of Norway, a member of NATO, and the capabilities of the Norwegian armed forces to operate in extreme cold, the special forces of Oslo exactly corresponded to the Pentagon's desires. "*It is completely*

normal that we participate in these operations, because we ⟨ part of NATO. Given that operations in Afghanistan are under N command, given that one of the members of the organizati the USA, was attacked, we have the obligation, following artic of the Atlantic charter, to help any country of NATO thus attacke This declaration of a member of the Norwegian government v well accepted by the Norwegian people and nobody protes against it.

In the best tradition of commando units, Norwegian army a navy Special Forces are capable of undertaking Long Range Rec naissance Patrols, close target reconnaissances and destruction

Above. A norwegian commando in a LUP somewhere in the South-Ea of Afghanistan. Norwegian SF are composed of the Land component of the Norwegian Army Special Operations Command (NORASOC) and the naval component of the Norwegian Special Operations Command (NORNAVSOC). Very few people realize that the Norwegi Special Forces were among the very first units to enter Pristina during the 1999 Kosovo war.

Left. On one of Task Force 180 advanced bases, a group of special forces operator board a 160th SOAR Chinook helicopter. Within NATC the Norwegians, and especially their special units, are universally recognized as the masters of the arctic environment. The Norwegian special naval unit is based in the North of the country, enduring very severe weather conditions, while their Army counterparts are located in the South of Norway, in a forested zone that is closer to the country's inhabited areas. In spite of those different locations, the two units follow a very similar training syllabus that tends to take them to the same training grounds.

Opposite page, top. A norwegian commando keeping moveme in a valley neighbouring Pakistan under close watch. During nine da in March 2002, the norwegian commandos, alongsides their Gern KSK and American SEALs colleagues, were ordered to sea and destroy "Al-Qaida" fighters South of the city of Gard

Opposite page, bottom. In the best Commando tradition, norweg Navy and Army Special Forces are equally at ease conducting L Range Reconnaissance Patrols, Close Target Reconnaissance, La target marking for the air forces, demolition of high value targ or intelligence gathering missions. *(Norwegian MOD pictur*

Norwegian Rangers

Called Fallskjermjegerkommandoen for paratrooper commando Rangers, the Norwegian army Special Forces are organized in a battalion-sized unit. Their missions consist of long range reconnaissance patrols in the depths of enemy territory, special OPs for the benefit of deep fire artillery units, direct action and forward air controlling and laser marking for the benefit of attack aircraft.

All Rangers are jump trained, a minority being also HALO/HAHO qualified as well as pathfinder trained.

The operations in Afghanistan gave the Norwegians the opportunity to deploy their specially modified Mercedes 290 GD 4X4 vehicles. The vehicle shown here is fitted with a ring mounted M2 HB Browning .50 calibre machine gun, smoke dischargers and side mounted racks loaded with fresh water and diesel fuel jerry cans.
(Norwegian MOD picture)

The Scandinavian Special Forces

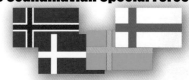

The Scandinavian countries, Denmark, Finland, Norway and Sweden, have a whole range of special units of limited sizes but that are all extremely capable of operating under the most severe arctic conditions. This explains the considerable interest shown by the US Command for those units as well as the repeated US requests to the various Scandinavian capitals. However, Finland and Sweden being neutral, only Denmark and Norway, as NATO members, answered the American requests.

Moreover, one cannot overlook the fact that for the first time in fifty-two years, the Atlantic organization used article 5 of the founding charter that stipulates that when one of the members is attacked (in this particular case, the USA with the September 11, 2001 attacks), the other members consider themselves as under attack too. This made a positive answer much easier for Denmark and Norway

Afghan villagers gathering to observe Norwegian operators who have just been inserted by an American helicopter. The Norwegian Special Forces contingent was called NORSOF TG and it first very discreetly arrived in Afghanistan during the first days of January 2002. Two different contingents were to serve each for three months in the south of Afghanistan under American command.
(Norwegian MOD pictures)

igh value targets. Furthermore, and that proved a very impor-
ant point, these units had worked for decades with their Ameri-
an, British and German NATO colleagues who were also present
n the Afghan mountains.

Arctic warfare specialists

"*I am proud to announce that a certain number of our special
forces are participating in operations in Afghanistan alongside the
Americans, as part of Enduring Freedom's military operations*",
declared Kristin Krohn Devold the Norwegian Minister of the Defen-
e, on January 8, 2002 "*and I have no doubt on their capabilities
o achieve excellent results*". This did not prevent the political oppo-

sition from attacking the government in April 2002, on the lack
of information concerning the special units and on the fact that
those units had to respect, during their missions in Afghanistan,
laws and international agreements.

At the end of June, two naval and army detachments returned
to Kandahar in order to prepare their equipment for the return to
Norway. One of the official reasons for the return was that the
Pentagon had asked them to take part in the campaign because
of their arctic skills and that, with the coming summer, this argu-
ment was wearing very thin. Others sources said that those very
small units would have been very hard pressed to provide a third
contingent in a row and that the ongoing operations no longer justified a permanent presence of the Norwegian contingent.

Because of their highly regarded mountain and arctic operations skills,
the norwegian special forces provided a much appreciated pool of expertise
to their American and British counterparts. Here, a norwegian two-man
team keeps track of enemy movements from a mountain top LUP.

Below. Norwegian special forces exiting an american SOCOM Chinook
helicopter during a search mission. The Norwegian Army and Navy special
forces contingents returned to Kandahar at the end of June 2002 in order
to pack their equipment and prepare for the move back to Norway.
One of the reason for that return was that the USA had asked for
norwegian assistance because of the arctic skills of their special forces and
that with arrival of summer, those skills were no longer needed. Another
explanation is that the dispatch to Afghanistan of a third contingent
stemming from such small units would have proved extremly taxing
for the different norwegian special operators. *(Norwegian MOD Pictures)*

Although the German army commandos were officially never supposed to hunt down the troops of Ben Laden and his allies, witnesses observed them, all the same, alongside members of the Australian SAS Regiment or American SEALs during search-and-destroy operations against "Al-Qaida" elements. In fact, reality was far removed from the declarations of the German government which was officially stating that their special forces were in charge of security in and around Kabul, within ISAF, the international force. It is true that this situation was rather embarrassing for Berlin, because to recognize this state of affairs was akin to recognizing that, for the first time since Second World War, German troops were actually taking part in combat operations.

Standing-by in Oman

In the beginning of December, 2001, the German government decided to answer favourably the requests for assistance from the Pentagon. Not wishing to send mountain troops, that are capable of operating in mountainous terrain but also lack any combat experience, it choose to employ the special units of Kommando Spezial Kräfte (KSK). Two weeks before Christmas, the first elements landed on the Bagram air base. Soon after, the first commando troops, with their light vehicles, were air transported by American C-17. At the beginning of January, the first operations could begin. At this time, several KSK troops had already been present in the region sin-

Above. In Kandahar, KSK operators during a vehicle patrol in the city. On e of the German operator is not taking any chance in this profound pro-Taliban city and his finger is resting on the trigger of his rifle. The KSK operator in the back of the vehicle is armed with a G36K fitte with an Holosight. *(Picture via Der Spiegel)*

Opposite page, top. KSK operator boarding an USAF C-130 in Bagra for an operation in the southeast of Afghanistan with Task Force Eve a TF made up of the Navy special forces, Norwegian and Danis special units. *(Bundeswehr Pictur*

Opposite page, in box. Badge of the DSO, the special operatio command which includes the KSI

Opposite page, far right. Insigne of the DLO, the airmobile comman with which the KSK operates mostl

ce October 2001. Indeed, they took part in the enormous Br tish exercise Swift Sword II / Saif Sareea in Oman, with thei British SAS and SBS counterparts and they then stayed in th region, just in case. The presence of German combat diver among the German vessels operating from Djibouti and Mom bassa in Kenya was also reported.

In March, the KSK commandos took part in *Operation Ana conda* alongside the US Navy SEALs and the Australian and Br tish SAS. In spite of constant tactical air support, this missio was difficult, mainly because of the ruggedness of the area o operation and the very tough and elusive enemy. At the en

AFGHAN MOUNTAINS

...f this operation, the KSK operators had not much to show for ...eir efforts but they had gained invaluable combat expe-...ence.

...n operations with the SEALs.

All together, two groups of a hundred commandos each ...perated one after the other in Afghanistan. Carrying only ...ght weapons that could, if necessary, be confused with tho-... of other American or British special units, the KSK opera-...rs were always transported by American helicopters, either ...om the Bagram airport or from the Kandahar airport. These two ...roups were made up of elements taken from the four rifle com-...anies commanded by an HQ troop. During this deployment, neigh-...ouring Uzbekistan was used as a rear-echelon base. This base was ...mposed of a command group (including some "reserve" soldiers) ...nd a logistical unit, the Luftwaffe transport aircrafts landing the-... first before finally reaching Bagram.

Considering the small size of this unit (four hundred and fifty ...eople according to official documents), the fact that two hundred ...mmando of the KSK operated in Afghanistan is quiet

KSK operator on patrol, Kabul area, 2002.
...nitially, the KSK were only supposed to provide close protection teams ...to some senior ISAF staff members in Kabul. This operator is dressed ...in the desert version of the famous German "Flecktarn" camouflage ...nd he is heavily armed with a G36C assault rifle, an HK USP P8 pistol ...and an HK 69 A1 40 mm grenade launcher, the ammunition of which being carried in an american grenadier vest.

Above.
A pair of German commando snipers. The KSK deployed more than one hundred fighters in Afghanistan from December of 2001 on. They participated in a large number of operations beside the other Special Forces in Task Force K-Bar in southeastern Afghanistan.
(Yves Debay Picture)

Panzerfaust 3-T

AWM

KSK ARMAMENT IN AFGHANISTAN

G-36

G-36 C

USP Compact

G-36 K

PDW

HK-69

Top. Abandoning their specially modified Mercedes Wolf light vehicles, the German special forces received from the Americans several Humvees which were somewhat modified in order to increase their speed and firepower.
(Picture via Der Spiegel)

Abo
On August 24th, 2002, the commander-in-chi
general Tommy R . Franks, congratulates c
of the KSK officers for the success encounte
during joint operations led in the So
of Afghanistan. *(DOD Pictu*

The KSK

The Kommando Spezialkräfte (KSK) is broken down in four rifle companies and a LRRP company. The operational companies are only made up of officers and non-commissioned officers. When missions away from Germany are undertaken, as it occurred in Afghanistan, the KSK can rely on three support companies: one signal company, one logistic and maintenance company, and a medical company.

Selection and training are the responsibility of the KSK school which is called the Ausbildung und Versuchszentrum (AVZ). The AVZ includes an engineer troop which is tasked with the development of different demolition charges and, in an operational situation, would be dispatched within the rifle companies.

The KSK selection course for officers (who can't be more than 30) and non-commissioned officers (28 - 32) lasts three months. The preselection tests are especially demanding, particularly extensive and they last several days.

During the three selection months, the candidates have to operate in different environments: "forest" in the Black Forest; "mountain" in Bavaria; and a "survival phase" in different locations. It is clear that this selection course is extremely demanding and only a very small number of volunteers manage to gain acceptance into its ranks.

Above. During Bright Star exercise in Egypt, the German command discreetly deployed a detachment of KSK operators in order to train them in desert environment. That training proved very valuable in Afghanistan less than year later.
(DOD Picture)

In box.
Cap badge of the KSK (*Kommando SpezialKrafte*).

KSK sniper.
During *Operation Anaconda*, numerous joint Coalition special forces teams were inserted on high grounds. Made up of a mix of US, British, Australian and German special forces, they wove a tight net around the mountains into which Taliban groups and the "Al Qaida" staff had fled. Snipers and tactical air control parties were tasked with the destruction of those enemy detachments. This KSK sniper is equipped with what is probably one of the best semi-automatic sniper rifle of the moment, the HK PSG-1. He is dressed in a mix of civilian and military clothes with desert Flecktarn trousers and a civilian fleece jacket.

Left.
The KSK detachment in Afghanistan was equipped with Mercedes
Wolf light vehicles modified by the addition of side-mounted
bins for water and fuel jerry cans as well as a roll bar.
The KSK was equipped with 5,56 mm G36K, 4,6 mm PDW as
personal protection weapon, MP5K and MP5SD, HK 69 40 mm
grenade launchers and Accuracy International G22
and HK PSG-1 sniper rifles.

Belo
Besides 4 x 4 Mercedes Wolf vehicles, the German commandos we
also equipped with modified Humvee. On the whole, two grou
of about a hundred operators each operated in two differe
by rotations in Afghanistan. Slightly armed (equipped), the elemer
of the KSK were transported by the American helicopters from Bagram
base and that of Kandahar during each of their operation
These two groupings were established (constituted) with elements take
among the four companies of fight, the frame assured (insure
from small ball of commar
(KSK Picture

**KSK operator during
an anti terrorist
operation.**
Germany did take part
in anti "Al Qaida" operations,
KSK commandos operating with
US Navy SEALs in a way far remote
from the official German government
stance. Uniforms worn on operations
were very different from what Bundeswehr
regulations permit, each operator favouring
effectivness over regulations.
The mixing of different
camouflage patterns was quite
characteristic of operations
in Afghanistan, a US desert
camouflage M-65 Field Jacket being
here worn over desert Flecktarn
german camouflage,
a bush hat and a local scarf
completing the "uniform".
The same leeway was to be found
on weaponry, from MP-5s to G-22s
(German version of the Accuracy
International AWM) with all the different
G-36 versions in between, the G-36C
being the most compact of the range.
On this reconstruction, the G-36C
is fitted with an Holosight
and the spare ammunition
are carried in a woodland-camouflage
copy of a TAC-V1 assault vest.
The secondary weapon is the regulation
HK P8 carried in a low-slung holster.

THE DANISH SPECIAL FORCES

Among the Task Force K-Bar operatives were two hundred Danish Special Forces from the JaegerKorpset and the FrömandsKorpset. They took part in numerous missions with the SEALs and the KSK paras.

Like the Norwegian and German commandos, the Danish arrived in Afghanistan at the end of December 2001, with their light Mercedes-Benz 290 GD 4x4s, some specially modified for the Special Forces, some not. However, given the nature of the terrain, they were heliborne for most of the main special operations, and later on foot !

THE TWO DEPLOYMENTS OF THE FRENC

At first, the media did not pay much attention to them and it's only several months after their return that the fact that several French special units had been sent to Afghanistan became common knowledge.

It is true that during their presence, the COS (French Special Operations Command) and DRM (Directorate for military intelligence) commandos were not involved in any direct combat actions. As of now, it is yet too early to know what the second batch of French operators will actually do when deployed on the ground. These soldiers are France's answer to the American administration's call for more troops for ISAF during the G8 summit of May 2003 in France. The plan is for 150 French special operators to be deployed in Afghanistan to take over from the Italian ISAF SF contingent.

Compared to its Nordic counterparts which sent more troops and took part in several combat operations from January 2002, (102 Danish commando, 103 German KSK special forces, 78 Norwegian Jegerkommandoen), the first French detachment that only was fifty operators strong was very modest. Among the often-quoted reasons for those differences were the facts that the French SF units were not send to carry out offensive actions and that they were not integrated into the various Task Forces of the Coalition. Indeed, the COS detachment always was under "Repfrance" (French contingent commander) authority for the whole of its deployment in Afghanistan.

Restricted and limited in its actions

In fact, everything began in October 2001, when the messen-

gers of the American government toured the Occidental capitals in search of specialized units capable of operating in extreme environments. If Berlin, Copenhagen, Oslo, Canberra, Ottawa and Wellington answered favourably and made their respective special forces ready, the reaction in Paris was different. No official stance was ever made public, but there are two plausible answers; either the French government did not trust its own COS units to such an operation or the same government considered they had not been given sufficient information and access to intelligence in order to give a well researched answer.

According to some, the President of the French Republic and the Prime Minister agreed to send special forces to Afghanistan with the coalition forces. Two plans were drawn by the Joint Staff;

the COS gathered its stand-by units in the Caylus training camp t start rehearsing possible scenarios; the DRM sent some liaiso teams to an unspecified Gulf state to liaise with the Americans

All those plans were to be countered by some of the Presiden t's advisors who thought that the COS was not ready for such ar operation and that they could easily be exchanged for some o the DGSE (Directorate for foreign security, specializing in unde cover and "deniable" actions) undercover agents that already wer operational in Afghanistan. To make matter worse, contradictor "lobbies" that tried to favour the use of a special unit against ano ther also disrupted the contingency planning. So, the Frenc government finally opted for the dispatch of line units to the Nort of Afghanistan reinforced with some COS close-protection and lia

PECIAL FORCES.

son teams which had no mandate to carry out offensive missions. That first display of French commandos to Afghanistan was thus remain very restricted in its scope and its action.

The Uzbek "hassle"

The COS unit that was sent to Afghanistan was split into three elements. They were known by their French acronyms of "EIT" for theatre (of operations) initial teams, the "ELC" for liaison and contact teams, and finally the "PATSAS" for SAS patrols (in memory of the French SAS regiment desert patrols of WW2 times), made up of 1st RPIMA paratroopers.

The arrival of French special forces was two-fold. First an ELC team landed in Mazar-e-Sharif; this team was made up Commando-Marine (Navy Commandos) belonging to the De Montfort Commando and of combat swimmers from the Commando Hubert under a CTP (Tactical Command Cell) staffed with FORFUSCO (French Naval Special Warfare Command). This detachment stayed in the North of Afghanistan from December 2001 until February 2002. It thus managed to avoid what was often referred to as the "Uzbek hassle" when, in November, 2001, a 21eme RIMa (Amphibious Infantry) company which was supposed to be deployed in Mazar-e-Sharif, was stuck by administrative and diplomatic red-tape in Uzbekistan for a month. The liaison and reconnaissance mission of this reduced detachment remained limited because the French contingent was rarely granted the authorization to leave the Mazar-e-Sharif airport zone they patrolled.

The second detachment

In the South of the country, the other detachment was made up of EIT, ELC and PATSAS teams that had arrived in Bagram in January 2002 in order to deploy in the Kabul area. This detachment, which was not connected either with the ISAF, or with the Coalition's forces but only with Repfrance consisted of operators belonging to the 1er RPIMa (Amphibious Paratroopers Regiment, the French Army SF Regiment), the 13th RDP (13th Airborne Dragoons, a LRRP unit highly appreciated by the American command for its skills) and the CPA 10 (Air Force Commandos). On January 17, two Orleans Squadron C-160 Transall transporting "EIT" teams and 1er RPIMa operators landed on the Kabul airport.

Their mission was to conduct discreet reconnaissance using 4X4 civilian SUVs in the Kabul region. On the other hand, the BATFRA (French battalion) mission still was to secure the Kaboul-

RECHERCHE ET SAUVETAGE AERO

R.E.S.A.L

SEARCH AND
RESCUE ON THE SUMMITS

eft. CPA-10 French Air Force commandos performing a training
andem jump from 2900 meters.

Previous page, bottom.
he RESAL French Air Force pilot rescue team during
training mission in the Tajikistan mountains.

Right. During their several months spent in Tajikistan,
the RESAL team performed several training jumps
in all sorts of conditions in order to be able to rescue
crew members in case of a crash.

Right, center. CPA-10 HALO/HAHO jumpers getting ready for a
high-altitude training jump over Kirghizistan.

Bottom, from left to right. Under the curious gaze of local Tajik civilians,
RESAL operators training on the rescue of wounded air force crewman
in a mountainous area. After having been stabilized, the crewman
would have been evacuated by helicopter. RESAL was the first
of such deployment for the French Air Force.
(Armée de l'Air Pictures)

From March, 2002, the French Air Force set up in Dushanbe,
ajikistan, a Search and Rescue or SAR team capable of helping
rench aircrews in high mountain areas. Indeed, France within the
ramework of *operation Héraclés* had set up a detachment consis-
ng of six Mirage 2000D which operated from Manas base in Kir-
hizistan. These attack aircrafts which operated over Afghanistan
ad to fly over hundred of kilometres of very high mountain, par-
cularly over the Pamir mountain range where some summits
ower at over 7 000 metres.

This team was called Resal (French acronym for air droppable
earch and rescue), and was made up of eighteen troopers. Part of
hat group was made up of Air Force Commandos belonging to the
ir Force CPA 10 airborne which belongs to the Commandement des
pérations Spéciales (French Special Operation Command). During
his deployment, the CPA10 commandos were placed under strictly
ir Force authority.

The Resal team was reinforced with two members of the Gendarmerie (French military police) mountain specialists belonging to the
eloton de Gendarmerie de Haute Montagne (PGHM) or High Moun-
ain Gendarmerie Platoon from Chamonix and Briançon in the French
lps, a doctor belonging to the CPA-10 and an Air Force communica-
on specialist.

If a Mirage 2000 D crew (pilot and weapon system operator) had
o bail out, the rescue mission would have been either flown in by
ajik Mi-8 helicopters or would have jumped in using HALO tandem
echniques since at least three CPA-10 operators were tandem-jump
ualified and able to jump with the PGHM or medical specialists. Once
e mission was completed and the crew rescued and stabilized the
esal would have had to reach a landing zone to be extracted by heli-
opter.In the end, the Resal team never had to intervene and after
even months of presence (from March 2 till September 30, 2002),
esal, the first in the Air Force, was de-activated.

Previous page, from top to bottom

The French Navy Task Force 473 took part in Operation *Heraclés*, cruising for months in the Gulf of Oman. At least twenty commando-Marine (French Navy special forces) took part in that mission. They had to be ready for boarding operations and were split into two teams, the assaulters belonging to Commando Jaubert and the snipers belonging to Commando de Montfort.
(Marine Nationale Pictures)

Right and below.
During the various visits of French and foreign dignitaries, COS close protection teams operating either in uniform or in civilian clothes and using discreet weapons were tasked with the body guarding of all sorts of VIPs.
(ECPAD Picture)

1er RPIMa paratrooper, Bamian area, 2002.
COS operators, especially those of the 1er RPIMa, were oten tasked, like their Delta Force comrades with close protection missions of Afghan dignitaries or visiting French VIPs. Operating in civilian clothes, the French BG were easy to distinguish from their US counterparts because they were the only one to use the FN P-90 SMG. The secondary weapon is the licence-built PA MAS G1, the French version of the Beretta 92F.

Bagram Main Supply Route. These intelligence gathering patrols were undertaken for the benefit of the commander of the French units of the ISAF, some of them going as far as Bamian in order to provide close-protection teams to various political personalities. The COS commandos and especially the 1st RPIMa paratroopers were involved in the discreet protection of the French embassy (that was also guarded by policemen) and of the various buildings occupied by French forces and civil servants.

Always present on the ground, the COS light teams have since the beginning of 2002 played the same liaison role with the different French units that have been deployed to Afghanistan.

A new deployment for the French SF

After the Evian G8 summit in June 2003, a French policy change was made public with the decision of the French government to send a 150 strong special forces detachment to Afghanistan within the Coalition's forces.

The French commandos were now going to operate within the special operation Task Force alongside the American troops in search of Taliban and of their allies. That decision was made easier by the keen interest displayed by the Americans about some specific French special forces units.

Contrarily to what has been asserted before, the French DGSE (General Directorate for Foreign Security, the French secret services) had no field agent inserted with the Northern Alliance on September the 11th. The only DGSE field agent who was anywhere near was the Turkmenistan/Azerbaijan/Tajikistan area station chief who could only tour the Northern Alliance operational areas every three months because he was gathering intelligence from French expatriate workers in the Duchambe area the rest of the time.

It is true that the French-Northern Alliance and especially the French-Major Massoud relations were going back a long way. France had been helping Massoud since the departure of the Soviets in 1988, more in words and official support from top French politicians (Massoud was officialy received in Paris in 2001) than in operational deeds like the Iranians or the Russians but still, this link was valued by both sides, no matter the colour of the political party in power in Paris.

Inspection visit

Just a few days after Massoud assassination and the terrorist attacks on the WTC and in sharp contrast to previous behaviours, the DGSE was ordered to send a dozen members from its Perpignan-based CIPS (Specialized Airborne Training Centre) and Roscanvel-based CPEOM (Specialized Maritime Operations Training Centre) to Afghanistan. Before those operators were dispatched to the area, General Rondot from the French Defence Minister Cabinet and himself a former member of the DGSE went on an inspection visit of the operational area in order to get a clearer view of the situation. He was closely followed by the DGSE deputy chief who followed on his tracks on a fact finding mission escorted by the first DGSE special operators. Those two groups worked separately.

The CPIS and CPEOM teams operated independently too but with similar missions albeit in different areas. Their main mission was to re establish old friendships that had been struck before with Northern Alliance leaders, front commanders and political chiefs who were emerging after Massoud's death. Those small teams, working alongside French intelligence in Pakistan, gathered a lot of high-value intelligence that were shared with the Americans who were eagerly waiting for them.

Game Over...

The French soon realize they must be quick because a first CIA team lands on the 26th of September, its pockets stuffed with hundreds of thousands of dollars that are quickly showered on the Northern Alliance commanders. Paris does not realize it at once but the game is then over for the French who are not ready to spend 70 million USD (that is the price the CIA paid for the Afghan campaign) on the Northern Alliance. One week latter, the DGSE teams have linked up with the main Northern Alliance commanders and they have grandly offered them a present: a GPS receiver each...When the American teams finally arrive and start setting up their equipment for the first air-delivery of tons of US military equipment, the choice of the Afghans on who to team up with to win this war is rather quick...From being mid-level players, the French soon became spectators who were rapidly told to stand aside. After reporting on this new situation to Paris, the DGSE operators followed the Northern Alliance into Kabul, searching a number of important "Al Qaida" buildings along their way.

By all accounts, the liaising mission was accomplished in time and efficiently, intelligence was gathered and shared with London and Washington but France quickly turned into a spectator as soon as full scale operations started.

(Yves Debay Picture)

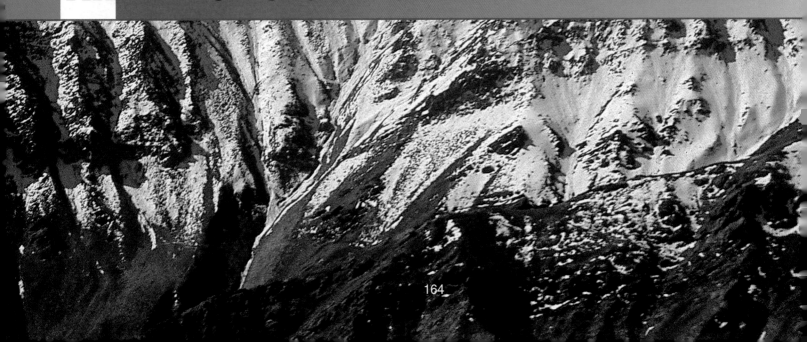

THE FRENCH SECRET SERVICES ACTION GROUP

Airborne Dragoon of the 13th RDP (Airborne Dragoons Regiment), January 2002.
The French special Forces in Afghanistan were discreet, the scope of their missions being very limited, at least during the first phase in spite of years of past military and cultural cooperation with the Afghans, before and after the Soviet era. The 13th RDP, with its unmatched experience in long range reconnaissance provided a sizeable part of the French detachment. The Afghanistan deployment was a good opportunity to test some new equipment like the "Guerilla" BDU in Central European camouflage which proved fairly well suited for the environment or the commercial "Elite" modular assault vest which can be compared to the US MOLLE. Armed with an HK MP5 SD6 SMG, this Dragoon carries with him all the necessary equipment for the forthcoming missions; water, batteries, radios, scopes...

THE ISAF'S SPECIAL FORCES

The mission of the special forces of Korps Commandotroepen (KCT) in Kabul is to patrol by night and by day in their light vehicle, here a modified 4 x 4 Mercedes G, and to provide intelligence to the commander of the Dutch detachment and the ISAF intelligence cell.
(Yves Debay Picture)

TURKISH SPECIAL FORCES

Turkey deployed a maximum of two Special Forces companies in the Kabul area; pictured here are commandos from the mountain brigade in Kabul. In 2002, when the ISAF was under Turkish command, the role of those commandos was increased. The presence in the central picture of a new 40 mm grenade launcher is interesting.
(Yves Debay Picture)

DUTCH SPECIAL FORCES

Those Dutch commando belonging to the Stoottroepen get ready before setting off on patrol. The special forces of the ISAF have a tough mission in their hand considering the sizeable number of hostile factions, the ever present risk of bomb or terrorist attacks and the latent hostility of a part of the population against all foreign armies. This mission is not made any easier by the military agreements that govern the presence of the ISAF and that are particularly restrictive. *(Yves Debay Pictures)*

The ISAF forces deployed around Kabul in 2002 represented eighteen different detachments, including four Special Forces units coming from the Dutch, Italian, Austrian and Turkish armed forces.

Covert special forces have also certainly been inserted within regular "line" units but too little is known about those discreet units to be specific. What is known is that, for example, the French detachment had no special unit within the BATFRA (French Battalion) but that the Repfrance (French representative) could count, in case of need, on a COS (French Special Operations Command) detachment that was deployed in the Kabul region The British used the same option with their SAS/SBS contingent located in Bagram.

Multiple threats

The Kabul Multi National Brigade (KMNB) commander could also count on a group of Special Forces numbering among them two hundred Dutch commandos from the 13th Infantry Battalion Stoottroepen, which landed in Afghanistan between January 21 and February 10, 2002. The mission of these special forces of the *Korps Commandotroepen* (KCT) was mostly to patrol in their 4 x 4 Mercedes G light vehicle. Those intelligence gathering missions were undertaken in answer to specific Dutch commanders requests or for the benefit of the ISAF intelligence cell which was hard pressed facing multiple threats against the coalition.

The Italian detachment that was to be relieved by 150 French COS operators in 2003 numbered 356 mostly originating from the Col. Moschin assault battalion and the airborne Folgore brigade.

The original mission of the Italian SF operators was to provide an intelligence gathering capability to the Italian contingent commander, to undertake reconnaissance missions directly under its control and to provide a quick reaction force in case of troubles.

On January 8, 2002, the Austrian government also decided to send a small SF detachment to join the other countries providing contingents to the ISAF.

This detachment was forty-five soldiers strong, stemming from two elite Austrian armed forces units, the *25th Jägerbataillon* and the *Zentrum Jagdkampf*. The latter can be compared to the British 22nd SAS Regiment; it specializes in deep

reconnaissance, sabotage and hostage rescue. The *25th Jägerbataillon* is the only light Austrian infantry unit specifically tasked with airmobile operations. After a week of mission preparation in the German Infantry School in Hammelburg alongside the 250 German sol-

ITALIAN SPECIAL FORCES

Left and opposite right.
Two pictures of Italian Carabinieri belonging to the Tuscania Battalion which is in charge of providing security for the ISAF Italian detachment as well as some special operators who work alongside their Col. Moschin in the Special Forces role. *(Yves Debay Picture)*

Bottom left. Close-up on a Dutch commando belonging to the Korps Commando troepen. He wears a mix of Dutch, French (Goretex jacket) and Canadian equipments. *(Yves Debay Picture)*

diers who had been earmarked for that mission the Austrian detachment was operational i Kabul on February 4, 2002. The mission of th Austrian commando was to provide protectio for some specific buildings, to protect foreig dignitaries visiting Kabul and to act as a contin gency force in case of a hostage-taking situa tion in the Afghan capital.

The Turkish Special Forces were represente by a commando company from the Mounta Brigade which arrived in mid-February 200. A second company reinforced this unit when Tu key took command of the ISAF in June 200.

According to some sources, the presence c Turkish Special Forces was nothing new sinc they are supposed to have been operating i Afghanistan from October 2001.

Unofficially, a hundred Turkish Special Fo ces operators are rumoured to have been se to Afghanistan in October 2001 and to hav played a discreet role alongside the Northe Alliance forces until the fall of Kabul.

Other sources claim that elements of th Uzbek and Tajik armies, operating more free in Afghanistan because they belong, like th Afghan, to the Moslem world, were present c the ground even before the Turks to support th Northern Alliance against the Taliban.

As far as the Turkish commandos were conce ned, their number rose from 250 in mid-Febru ry 2002 to almost 500 in July of the same yea During several months, they operated with th British units in the First district, a high-risk zo that was previously under strict Taliban contr. At present, the Dutch commandos are in contr of this area because the deputy commander the ISAF is Dutch.

A very limited mandate

In a difficult context, faced with a very pro population that has never appreciated foreig armies on its soil, limited by very strict Rules Engagement (ROEs) the ISAF's Special Forc mission scope was and remains very reduce indeed.

The stress officially put on the political so ving of all problems by the Amid Karzaï gover ment does not make the mandate of these sp cial units any easier.

SPECIAL FORCES IN AFGHANISTAN - WAR AGAINST TERRORISM

SPECIAL FORCES IN AFGHANISTAN - WAR AGAINST TERRORISM

Acknowledgments

The author wishes to thank the following persons for their help and their time spent in researching documents, material and equipment : Cyrill d'Agata, Pierric Boudehen, Philippe Bourotte, Gilles Garnier, Laurent Jurquet, Thierry Roger (TR Equipements) and Denis Wittner.

Special thanks go to David Shadok, the efficient coordinator of the photography sessions.

Special acknowledgments are also due to Laurent Ciejka, who inspired a special issue of RAIDS which was so successful that it was turned into this book.

Thanks to Janice Lert for additional translation and to Cyril Lombardini for his encylopedic knowledge.

The photographs would not have been possible without the help of the Etablissements Maratier, a French company specializing in rental of weapons and film accessories.

The author also wishes to thank Marianne Baroso of SIPA-Press, Per Holby of the public relations service of the Norwegian Armed Forces, and the military office of the Norwegian Embassy in Paris, Simone Heyer of the Australian Army magazine "Army".

Supervision, and lay-out : Jean-Marie MONGIN.
© Histoire & Collections 2003

Published by
HISTOIRE & COLLECTIONS
SA au capital de 182 938, 82 €

5, avenue de la République
F-75541 Paris Cédex 11 - France
Téléphone 01 40 21 18 20
Fax   01 47 00 51 11

ISBN: 2-913903-90-8

Publisher's number: 2-913903

© Histoire & Collections 2003

This book has been designed, typed laid-out and processed by Histoire & Collections and the Studio Graphique A & C entirely on integrated computer equipment Photogravure. Studio A & C Printed by Zure, Spain, European Union August 2003